Write for the

Religion Market

John A. Moore

An ETC Publication

Library of Congress Cataloging in
    Publication Data

Moore, John Allen
    Write for the religion market.

    Bibliography: p. 124
    1. Religious literature—Authorship.   I. Title.
BR44.M66   808'.0662   80-25607
ISBN 0-88280-084-1

Published by ETC Publications
Palm Springs
California 92263

Contents

To my wife
Pauline Willingham Moore

Foreword

This book is addressed to all of you who would like to write for the religion market, whether news, features or any other type of material that is used.

It is assumed that you have no formal training, perhaps also no special talent, in writing.

If you are willing and able to work at it with some regularity, you can achieve a degree of success in this fascinating field.

In the event that you do find yourself in this elite group of the committed, welcome aboard—and happy writing!

John Allen Moore

One

Would You Like To Be A Writer?

Martin Luther is reported to have said, "The art of printing is God's newest and greatest gift to help us advance the work of the gospel." No one can accuse Luther of not making use of the press. He was the leading pamphleteer of his age, writing for the religion market; and his works can fill a hundred volumes.

In our day, news stands and book stores are flooded with printed material, but much of it we would be better off without. Writings of a specifically religious character are relatively scarce in daily newspapers and general magazines, although the editors would in many cases be glad to print more of such material if it were prepared according to their needs. We do not take full advantage of the gift of printing as Luther did in his time.

Let us not think the printed word is on the wane, however, superseded by radio and movies then television. People read more than ever before. Editors of church periodicals, daily newspapers and secular journals look hopefully in their mail each morning for suitable articles and stories which they can publish. Would you like to help meet this need? You can.

Yes, you can. If you are able to read the pages of this book, if you can write decent business letters or correspond with your friends, you can write for publication.

I do not predict that you will become a great author. I do not say you will produce literature in the classical sense. I say only that you can find your place somewhere in the broad field of religion writing. You can prepare material which will be gratefully received and published by editors, even paid for.

Not all of it, of course. Even big-name writers cannot generally count on everything they write being published. Unless you find employment as an editor or news reporter, you will be a "free-lance" writer. This means that each effort will be accepted for publication or rejected according to the editor's estimate of its worth and his own needs at the time.

This may make for uncertainty of income, but as a free lance you will probably be a part-time writer also. This brings with it the advantage of not being dependent on the editor's decision for your livelihood. Free lancing gives you a built-in measure of progress. You are encouraged as more and more of your work is accepted.

How can I say that almost anyone reading this could write for publication? If all readers became writers, would it not flood the market and drive editors to distraction? From such a dread state they are protected by the "if." Most readers of these words will probably not become writers for publication. All too few of you will.

The reason is that there is one more condition, if you want to be a writer. You must work at it. Wishing and dreaming will not suffice. If it did, almost all readers *would* be writers, for they envy the authors of best sellers whose fame and fortune *seem* so easily won. Successful writers use the tools familiar to all of us—words, paper, a typewriter. *We* also think up things and speak prose every day. What could be simpler than writing down our thoughts and becoming famous?

If this is as far as your desire to be a writer goes, you need not read any further. You can want to be a writer without

8

really wanting to write, for writing is work.

There seems to be a large company of those, however, who have counted the cost to some extent at least and still want to write. They feel they really have something to say but never get around to putting it on paper. They dream about writing, read about it and talk about it, but produce nothing for publication. How can they become writers, part-time free-lance writers, along with their daily work?

The satisfactions are great, for those willing to pay the price. Everyone who has a spark of individuality gets satisfaction out of making things—a cathedral or a bird house, an oil painting or a pleasing photograph, a trip to the moon or a win in the hundred-yard dash, a great oration or a clever turn of phrase in conversation.

The writer makes things also. The playwright, for instance, makes plays, as a wheelwright used to make wheels. The poet chooses his words for painting a picture in the lyric as the artist does his oils for a composition on canvas. The novelist builds his story from the materials of life. The same processes are at work in producing nonfiction except that the writer is bound to choose materials for his work of art from ideas and available facts.

As for preparation you may need to brush up on elementary principles of composition. Surely you will want to work on vocabulary, not only increasing the number of words at your command but practicing more precise usage.

Don't neglect the reading of good literature, more or less of classical rank, as well as reading widely in the type of material you intend to write. Make the most of writing assignments you may have in school or give to yourself. Keep a writer's diary maybe, with descriptions of your observations and thoughts each day. Write lots of letters and rewrite to make them good—straightforward and natural-sounding for you, but good.

Take a course or two in writing if available, attend writer's workshops, read some books and magazines on the subject if you will.

Regardless of how many or how few of these opportunities are open to you, the most important part of your preparation is the writing itself; don't wait about this until you do the other things. You learn to write by writing. The biggest roadblock for the beginner is that he or she will be content with reading and listening and talking and planning about writing. Afraid one has not learned enough to begin, he or she continues to read and to listen and to talk and to dream; there's nothing, not publication anyway, at the end of this road.

You must discipline yourself mercilessly, with a certain amount of time spent regularly in writing each week. Better, each day. And beware of allowing this time to be stolen by other claimants, even by books and magazines on writing.

Where can you find the time? In the same place you do for anything else, in the twenty-four hours we all have each day. If you are serious about writing, it must have precedence over many other things you have considered pleasurable, expected of you or almost essential.

You may have to spend less time watching television or listening to music, in aimless conversation or reading the newspaper, waiting idly for the bus or plane or attending unnecessary meetings. You must learn to stick with your typewriter, in the time sacred to writing, even if numerous chores beckon. If you wait until all the other things are attended to, the time for writing will be gone, day after day, with nothing to show for it.

Make a weekly schedule. Mark off your eight hours for sleep, time spent at your job and in church activities, some hours with the family or in recreation.

What do you have left? Here's what you have: your time for being a part-time free-lance writer. Choose a quiet place somewhere, or a place even if it is not quiet, and keep your appointment there conscientiously.

How much time? It depends on your purpose, as well as your necessary commitments. If you are content just to make a minor hobby of your writing, two or three hours a week will enable you to turn out a short piece now and then. If you are eager to make a real contribution in the writing field, you may want to devote that much time to it almost every day.

Anthony Trollope, popular English novelist of the nineteenth century, averaged more than a book a year by giving two hours to his writing before going to work at the post office each morning.

Start with an orderly method of work, but don't overdo it or even the tidying up and other incidental chores can gobble up the time that should go to writing.

Gather material carefully, write it up with sincerity and enthusiasm, then rewrite it until it is the best you can make it. Use a typewriter throughout if possible, and by all means do so for the final copy. If you do not type, and don't want to learn (you can teach yourself), send the material to one of the typists that advertise in writers' magazines.

If your article or story is returned by the editor you send it to, dispatch it to another and another and another, if you still consider the piece to be of value, with whatever rewriting seems to be called for each time. I once sold an article, which I believed in, on its eighteenth trip out.

Two

Begin With The Event

Where should you begin, in your avocation of writing for publication? You can start almost anywhere. You may want to try your hand at fiction, or in the preparation of an article about some person (maybe yourself), place or institution with which you are familiar. More modestly, you might start by writing a short "filler" giving some interesting bit of information or by sending in one of those "letters to the editor" of a newspaper or magazine which you read.

One of the best ways to begin is by reporting news events. This will hardly be for a leading daily to start with, rather perhaps a suburban or small-town weekly, your denominational paper or even a bulletin put out by your local church. Don't wait for a definite assignment; editors are happy to receive accurate news reports from any source.

What are the qualifications? The editor of a daily paper once said that in hiring members of his staff he assumed a reporter should be able to express himself clearly. Beyond that, the editor added, he would ask only that the reporter have curiosity, common sense and initiative. The same qualities characterize the free-lance writer.

"The greatest thing a human soul ever does in the world," said John Ruskin, "is to see something and tell in a plain way what he saw."

First you have to see it. It is surprising how superficial

most of us are as observers, and how inexact. Ask several persons to report a single occurence which all have seen and notice how different the accounts. As a writer make the hymn, "Open My Eyes That I May See" your theme song, and don't forget the verse beginning, "Open my ears that I may hear."

A good memory helps, of course. Develop it as much as you can. But don't depend on it exclusively. Take notes as you gather material and develop a simple filing system for clippings and other useful items.

Begin your writing, then, with the news. But what is that? It is concerned with some happening or situation or statements that are of interest to people. What makes it interesting from the standpoint of editors and news analysts who are responsible for deciding what is to be printed or reported on the air?

Crack reporters have, it is said, a "nose for news." They can smell it a mile away. Other people seem to be at a complete loss in choosing what to tell the public about. Asked to report in 150 words what happened at his church on Sunday, the local pastor might come up with a bony outline of his sermon. For journalistic purposes, this would be next to worthless—my apologies to the brother and his sermon!

Once I received, as director of an international religious press service, the report of a national student conference. It listed the entire roster of new officers for the student organization but gave no identifications and had not a single word about the program. The report could not of course be used for a press release.

Upon investigation it was discovered that the program had featured a music workshop with participants learning and presenting a cantata under the direction of its composer. Another workshop group, directed by a leading dramatist, produced a play. Both cantata and play were based on Jesus' parable of workers in the vineyard, which provided the theme for the conference.

A student in my journalism class dug up these facts, along with interesting information with which to identify several of the newly elected officers. There was news in the event, but it was not discovered and reported until one who knew what to look for was assigned to ferret it out.

It would not be easy to give a satisfactory definition of news, and even if we succeeded it would probably not be very helpful for the beginning writer. It ought to be a bit of assistance, however, to point out some newsworthy characteristics. No news story will have all those mentioned here, but if an event possesses several of these qualities it is surely news.

Timeliness. News must be new. It is not like salted pork but more comparable to fresh fruit, delicious but highly perishable—maybe the most perishable commodity on the face of the earth. This is especially true in our day when it takes not months but seconds to send messages around the world.

How recent does the event have to be in order to be classified as news? This depends to a great extent on where it is to be published. The editor of an afternoon daily may reject an item which tells of something that happened a few hours before because of a short piece about it in the morning papers. Correspondents for the general international news services consider that they have a "deadline every minute" as they compete with one another in reporting "hard" news (that regarded as important, urgent and of general interest) from around the world.

In most religion journalism speed is a good principle but not tyrannical law. Except for the press services, where every day counts, deadlines come once a week or once a month as a rule, according to the publishing schedule of each journal. Still, these deadlines must be known and observed. It is unforgivable in reporting for a religion newspaper, as any other, that a news item must be put in the next issue, or rejected, when it ought to be in the current issue.

The thing that counts is not necessarily when the event occurred but, in some cases, when it became known. One of the big religion stories a generation ago was the discovery of the Dead Sea Scrolls. This was exciting news although it dealt with manuscripts about two thousand years old and a sect of Jews that passed from the scene of history many centuries ago. The discovery itself was a newsworthy event of the highest order, followed by others as the full significance of the material became evident.

The greatest single problem faced in the press service mentioned above was impressing on volunteer reporters in various countries the need for promptness in sending in news. I received reports of national conventions as much as a month or more after the event. By that time the information was worthless for our purpose. An exception to this principle would be reports that filtered out of China or some other restricted land, which were welcome even if very late. There is no excuse for such tardiness where there are normal facilities of communication and freedom for sending factual reports.

Timeliness applies to announcements about coming events as well as those in the past. There may occasionally be need for a story on something planned for a year or more afterward, if it is of great significance to many people, but generally announcements are concerned with events planned for the immediate future.

Proximity. "Nearest-dearest," says an old German proverb. This applies to news. Reports from the immediate area or group concerned take precedence, other things being equal, over news from afar.

Local newspapers give preference to local news, and this provides a great opportunity for churches to make their work known—the opening of a new chapel, the coming of a new pastor or visiting speaker, revival services, concerts, a drama, youth camp, building plans, major renovations or a fine new organ. Probably none of these things would interest the editor of a national publication—or any paper published a hundred miles away—but the editor of your local paper will likely be delighted to get reports on such developments.

Don't expect professional newspersons to be sent to report such events. Newspaper staffs are usually not large enough to cover all these happenings. Unless you or someone else in your church assumes responsibility for getting the facts and takes the trouble to write them up in the way desired by the editor, these things will not be generally known. This is your opportunity.

Magnitude. Church people frequently come together in large numbers for rallies, conventions and conferences. These gatherings are newsworthy because many persons are concerned. Even in the most staid and conservative groups, something of interest is likely to happen when so many people are together, speeches made, projects presented, votes taken and leaders chosen. Those directly involved, their kin, neighbors, friends and many others want to read about what occurred.

Beware of thinking that the general reader's point of view

will be the same as that of a fellow believer in the group immediately concerned. Try to find that which would be of interest to and of significance to an outside observer and feature that, if you are writing for a daily newspaper or general periodical.

Sometimes interest centers in sheer numbers and size. A convention was the largest ever. A particular delegate was the oldest or youngest or tallest, or he traveled farthest to attend. A chapel is the most diminutive or a church has the highest steeple, the largest clock or the biggest budget. Somebody has attended church or Sunday school for a very long time or memorized a large part of the Bible. A pastor has baptized more people or conducted more funerals than almost anyone else around.

Any of these things may be newsworthy, especially at some point when a particular milestone is reached—30 years in attendance, 3,000 baptisms or 30,000 at a meeting.

Prominence. Almost anything evangelist Billy Graham says or does is news, due to his prominence in the world of religion. A position taken by the Pope, the ecumenical council of churches or leaders of a national association of evangelicals is also, for the same reason. Locally, a strong stand taken by a prominent pastor or rabbi on some political issue would be news, because of his position. A public Christian testimony by the mayor might be newsworthy also, due to his prominence in the community.

Denominational and other religion publications will be interested to publish, in addition to much of that mentioned above, reports of action taken by presidents and other leaders of national and state organizations, heads of theological seminaries, important boards and committees.

People are news, it is said. Certainly the leaders are.

Check regularly with them and you will have stories enough to keep you busy.

Places and material objects can have prominence too. Everyone knows about the White House, Hyde Park, the Berlin Wall. Some time ago I read interesting reports about commemorative meetings in Paulerspury, England. an insignificant village itself, it had importance for the evangelical reader even in faraway lands because the pioneer missionary William Carey was born there.

Doubtless there are places in your vicinity which are of local importance at least and it is likely there will be occasional celebrations or other newsworthy happenings in connection with them that will give you a "news peg" on which to hang the whole story.

Drama. Conflict, or at least some difference of opinion, seems to be inherent in almost any activity involving more than one person. Even when there is only one, there may be conflict with the forces of nature or with conscience. Conflict is assumed to be necessary in fiction, but it is sometimes just as important in factual writing.

Controversy, especially among people of prominence and on issues of importance, is newsworthy. Certainly no religion journalist should stoop to the muckraking tactics of irresponsible newspapers that are determined to make everything sensational. But where religious people earnestly disagree, there must be an issue which would interest and perhaps profit others. In any case, controversy is a part of church life as of other life and if the public or the larger fellowship of Christians or Jews considers itself involved, at least as concerned observers, people probably have a right to know the facts.

There seems to be a strong tendency in church circles (and others) to get all possible publicity so long as it is definitely favorable. There is often the effort to suppress, however, any report revealing that churches are composed of imperfect human beings. This causes editors of some secular papers to shy away from religion news. They find it next to impossible to get the full story. All they hear about is sweetness and light, and they know this cannot be the whole of it.

When we reveal only the nicest things about ourselves and our group, people begin to doubt even those good reports that happen to be true.

Reporters and editors must of course exercise restraint along with the best judgment they are capable of. The *New York Times* says it publishes "all the new that's fit to print," and it is quite true that some happenings are such that news of them is not fit to print. In religious journalism, however, fault is more likely to be in withholding news simply because it does not show church or temple people at their best than in publishing what is not fit to print as do so many secular journals today.

The decision for honest reporting should be made in principle and courageously adhered to, without raising the question of effect on public relations in regard to every particular piece of news. The free press has proved itself essential for civil democracy. It is just as necessary in the world of religion if our news agencies and periodicals are to be anything more than dispensers of publicity propaganda from the churches.

Consequence. How much is involved in the event you are considering for a possible news story? A discussion in the women's group of the local church as to whether the quarterly business meeting should be next week or the following will not rate space in the newspaper because the issue is of no consequence so far as most of its readers are concerned.

A decision by the same group to organize a giant rally and parade to oppose legislation legalizing the lottery, or for religious exercises in public schools, would be news. The actual carrying out of the plans would be even more newsworthy. The raising of a large fund by church young people for the support of a Cameroon student in the local college would be news also, at least in a small town weekly and church papers.

A theological seminary dismissed one of its professors. Normally such an event would be of significance mainly to the limited group of persons immediately concerned. But this was not an isolated happening. It had roots in action taken by the denomination several months before, because of a book written by the professor which was considered too liberal. Committees were appointed to investigate questions of orthodoxy. People talked openly of a possible split among the churches. Many persons were involved and likely to be affected in a serious way, and this became the top news story of the year in the denomination's many papers.

Not always in such a dramatic fashion, but in some degree, important news events have this quality of consequence. They are not isolated occurrences but rooted in past happenings, and they will probably be related to others yet to come. Unimportant items often stand alone, and if they are omitted from the day's news they are not missed. Not so those of great consequence.

It is a relative matter, of course. On the local church or temple scene, many people are affected to some degree and the event is of importance when one minister, priest or rabbi leaves and another comes, when a couple is married or a community center is established.

Emotion. Sometimes an event is not important in sheer news value but still makes an interesting story which will be read with appreciation. The emotional impact may be quite mild, as in the story about a group of children who must wait on the roadside in all kinds of weather without shelter for the Sunday school bus. Or it may be tremendous as in the story of the town beggar who is critically injured in saving the little son of the minister of music in a local church from a careening truck whose brakes had failed.

This kind of report is often referred to as the human interest story. It may be concerned with children, the handicapped or elderly persons. Sometimes its main characters may not be human at all. A brief story appeared in the Louisville *Courier Journal* about a nameless old dog of mixed breed, almost blind, that lived a on a certain street of the city. He molested no one, got his food from friendly householders up and down the street.

An outsider turned him in to the dog pound, and he was to be chloroformed. The newspaper story and accompanying photo of the animal brought many protests from irate readers. They objected in no uncertain terms to the dog's being put away. Several offered to take him. He got a nice home in which to pass the remainder of his days, as reported in the paper later in the week.

Nothing of great consequence or world-shaking importance in this, but it was of sufficient interest for the big city daily to give front page space to it for several days.

Humor. Stories which are primarily of interest for their humor fall also into the category of those which are generally unrelated to yesterday's news or tomorrow's. Any particular one could be omitted without great loss. But a story of this type now and then does much to please readers.

Don't think of humor just as jokes. One news release that was used by many papers told of a pastor whose "speech" at a convention consisted entirely of the Sermon on the Mount quoted from memory with considerable effect. Immediately afterward there were some interesting moments at the booth where convention speeches were being sold. Several delegates hurried to the booth and asked for a copy of this speech. They were chagrined when told they could find the "speech" word for word in their Bibles!

Unusualness. This may be regarded as the basic quality of almost any news. When a dog bites a man that is not news, old newsmen used to say, but if a man bites a dog that is news. There is a type of story, however, that is chiefly of interest because it is quite out of the ordinary, odd.

Orvil Reid, a missionary serving in Mexico, had finely developed lungs and chest muscles. On evangelistic tours and in schools he often began the service by lying face upward on the platform before his audience, a large stone being placed on his chest. A strong man then took a heavy sledgehammer and crashed one hefty blow after another on the rock until it broke into two or more pieces. Another part of Reid's program, out in the yard, was to have a truck drive over his chest, while he sang a hymn. When the time came for his testimony, he never lacked for listeners, according to published accounts.

A city daily featured stories about a seminary student, a candidate for foreign service as a medical missionary, who discovered he was able to foretell events. He could indicate in advance, news and feature stories claimed, who was going to win a race or other contest, which team would come out on top in a forthcoming game or tournament. He was careful to use his skill, he said, in such a way that it could not be capitalized on by gamblers, putting his prediction in a sealed envelope and locking it in a bank vault until after the event.

This was an unusual hobby for a seminarian, and it made news.

You might find a story in some unusual meeting place for a church, an uncommon occupation from which a pastor came into the ministry, strange hobbies among the membership. The realm of nature and animal life may provide odd circumstances to report—a peculiar place on church premises chosen by birds for their nests, a dog that attends services regularly or a tree that is growing through the boy's club hut.

Three

Writing The News Story

"The Middletown team won 7 to 6," would be a natural way for you to greet your friend after the game if he had been prevented by illness or otherwise from attending.

If you started out describing the crowd in attendance, condition of the field, uniforms of the players, music by the band, the starting lineup then the kickoff and on through the game, you would only exasperate your friend and make him sicker still. He would gladly listen to all the details but *only* after you report to him that vital piece of information which you have and he does not, the final score.

It is the same in news writing. Contrary to the order in features, fiction and spoken address, the news story should usually give the gist of the matter at the very beginning. Background and details are filled in after the main points have been stated.

This structure of the news story is often illustrated by the inverted pyramid or triangle. The wide base at the top represents the most important facts and the sides slanting to a point at the bottom stand for the details of decreasing importance.

The inverted-triangle method for writing the news story has distinct advantages. It is helpful for the busy editor. With worldwide communication systems bringing in news every hour, day and night, the editor of a modern newspaper or newscast is anxious to include stories about last minute developments. This means he must be able quickly to scrap or shorten material he had planned to use in order to make place for important news that arrived shortly before the deadline.

Since church news is almost always in the "soft" category, it will be just about the first to get the axe. The decision as to whether your story is just to be shortened or omitted entirely will likely depend on how it is written.

Shortening is easy if the story is so constructed that the editor can cut it from the bottom according to space available. If on the other hand it is written like fiction with climax near the end, or in a straight chronological order, all must be completely rewritten. There is just not time for this in a newspaper office as the deadline time approaches.

The publishing of news according to the inverted triangle is helpful also for the busy reader. Normally he will not have time to read the newspaper in its entirety, unless he is to resign his job and give full time to it. Some papers, especially the Sunday editions, have as much reading matter in a single issue as is contained in a fairly large set of books. It is hard for the newspaper reader to know which parts he wants to spend his time with if he has only the headlines by which to judge the contents.

If he can get the gist of the story by reading a few lines at the beginning, however, he knows whether to read on. Those giving an account of events which are of particular interest to him, he reads to the end. Others, in which he has mild interest, he follows halfway down. Even with the remainder he may read the lead sentences, in order to be informed to some extent about all newsworthy occurrences that are reported.

How do you as a free lance writer tackle the job of getting the facts about some event across to your reader?

First comes the leg work. As you cover the event, observe, listen, talk with those in position to know and accurately jot down the information you get. Check perhaps in newspaper files (the "morgue"), your own reference materials or those in libraries such as periodicals, almanacs and yearbooks to supplement identifications and background. Gather the facts, wherever they are to be found.

What facts? Reporters have six questions they ask themselves about a happening. Rudyard Kipling put them into verse:

> I keep six honest serving men,
> They taught me all I know.
> Their names are What, and Why
> and When,
> And How, and Where, and Who.
> I send them over land and sea,
> I send them east and west . . .

When the reporter has answers to the five W's and the H he feels he can write the story in a complete and satisfying form. The Who or What, When and Where will be in almost every story. Sometimes the Why and How are self evident, as when a church calls a minister. Occasionally some of the answers are unavailable. But the newsperson must always raise the questions, for one's self at least, in order to be sure some important angle is not being omitted.

In organizing your story, decide first on the opening or lead (pronounced "leed"). This should generally summarize the main facts. It may be one or more sentences, depending on the length and complexity of the story. The lead should usually take account at least of the Who or What, When and Where.

If more than one sentence is called for in the lead, do not hesitate to use two or three. A common fault of beginners is to manufacture a sentence monstrosity, trying to say everything at once. As an editor of the *New York Times* once expressed it, they write as if every first sentence were their last.

Almost never will the When and the Where be the very first items in the lead, although they may be in the "dateline" (this initial listing of place and date is not always used, especially the date part). Unless the When and Where are of importance for some special reason, they will generally be tucked away, perhaps at the close of the opening sentence or later, for the record.

When you have written a good lead for your news story the battle is half won. Copy writers often spend as much time on this as on all the rest. Sometimes you may write out and discard a dozen possible leads before finding one which just suits the story.

In deciding which of the principal facts to put in the very first place, that is, how to begin the lead itself, you might ask yourself the usual questions.

A What lead might begin as follows:

> An increase of 15 percent in gifts to the Home and Foreign Mission Fund by churches of the state was reported to the state convention board at its meeting in Ridgeville last week.

Who:

Montreat, N.C., Nov. 30—
Evangelist Billy Graham plans four

crusades in the U.S., and two abroad next year, according to the information given reporters here today.

Where?

The new residential community of North Benton was without a church of any kind until the organization of Faith Bible Church there last Sunday.

When?

A minute before midnight Sunday, the last day of the year, is the deadline set for the raising of $200,000 by Parkview Presbyterian Church to begin construction of its new educational building.

How?

"I write five new words on my mirror each morning and learn them while I shave," said Dave Barker, missionary to Nigeria, yesterday in explaining how he learns the Yorba language.

Why?

To show how U.S. Protestant ministers feel about proposed abortion legislation, the U.S.

Protestant Ministers' Fellowship is
polling its nationwide membership
on the question, a spokesman for
the organization stated in
Washington.

Sometimes a lead may begin with a direct quotation, as in
the How lead above, with a question or a striking
statement. More common is the summary lead or indirect
quotation, which may include directly quoted words or
phrases.

Another way to start is with the 1-2-3 lead, which is
preceded by an introductory statement to indicate general
content of the story:

United Methodist Bishop James
Martinow declared in an address to
the area conference of his church in
Bradbury last evening that
* Christians must make their
voices heard in Civic affairs.
* The Church should do more
for public morality.
* Christian brotherhood and
mission go together.

As for arrangement of material following the lead it might
help, in the beginning, if you write out each bit of
information on a separate slip of paper, then arrange the
slips according to your judgment and write up the story.

The inverted triangle is a good basic form, suitable for
most news stories, but it should not bind you in a
straitjacket. Sometimes the suitable form will more nearly
resemble a rectangle with all the facts of about equal

importance. Occasionally the upright triangle might represent the order.

Climax-at-the-end stories, usually brief, are almost always of the "soft news" type, whimsical, humorous or strongly human-interest. One I noticed in a daily newspaper described a would-be purse-snatcher descending on an old lady and ended with her chasing him down the street beating him over the head with her cane.

Whatever the form, make your story factual and objective. Be careful to avoid "editorializing" it. This includes not only direct comment and evaluation by the writer but even single words and phrases reflecting opinion such as "the finest program ever," "sincere prayer," "an inspiring message by a faithful servant of God." Such attributes may well be included if correctly attributed to some source. Otherwise the writer is responsible for them, and he or she should stick to observable or audible facts in a news story.

Example of the news story (announcement):

> Westport Road Chapel, sponsored by the Wesleyan Methodist Church of Piedmont, will begin services Sunday November 5 in a residence which has been adapted for church purposes. This announcement comes from the Rev. M. T. Aiken, minister of the church.
>
> The Rev. Charles J. Durham, a recently retired minister who is a member of Wesleyan Methodist, will serve as pastor of the chapel.

He is also to direct the community center which will provide clothing distribution and other social services at the chapel.

Seven Wesleyan Methodist families form the nucleus of membership in the new chapel, explains Mr. Aiken. Various offices in the new congregation and its church school are divided among them.

In addition to church school and worship service each Sunday morning, the chapel will have a Bible study hour on Wednesday evenings, says Mr. Aiken. Women of the Westport Road community are invited to a meeting in the chapel each Monday afternoon. A club for boys and one for girls are to be organized, and athletics will be included in their programs.

The chapel's building is located at 2375 Westport Road. It provides an auditorium to seat about a hundred persons, and several smaller rooms.

"There are abundant opportunities for enlargement of program and facilities," says Mr. Aiken. "It is anticipated that the congregation will later become an autonomous church."

A beginner might come up with something like the following for his first draft. Would this be acceptable?

The Wesleyan Methodist Church pastor, Rev. Aiken says his church is evangelistic and wants to start new churches. The local Wesleyan Methodist Church of Piedmont split off from the Methodist Episcopal Church, South. Northern and Southern Methodists united in 1939 and the United Methodist Church was formed in 1968.

One community that really needs a mission is the outer Westport-Road area. The people are quite poor, many unemployed, and there is great need for social work, distribution of clothing and so on. "The Wesleyan Methodists here are as interested in social work as United Methodists are," comments Rev. Aiken.

This will be done on premises of the new chapel at 2375 Westport Road. The large house that has been bought there has had walls knocked out so that one room can seat a hundred persons.

Rev. Durham, who was a pastor of a church at Cornishville and had a wonderful ministry there until his retirement in 1978, belongs to

Piedmont Wesleyan Methodist Church, and they elected him to pastor the new chapel. He will also superintend the social work.

Six other families—the Beavers, the Catletts, the Everetts, the Grants, the Mortons and the Tournages—will help Rev. Durham in the mission.

Rev. Don Aiken says, "I am very happy at the beginning of this mission, the establishment of the chapel and so on. There are abundant opportunities for enlargement of program and facilities. It is anticipated that the congregation will later become an autonomous church. I think every church should have one or more missions, then start another as soon as these become churches."

Rev. Durham agrees with Rev. Aiken and says he is prepared to give full time to work in the new location as long as this is needed, with little or no remuneration.

Mrs. Everett, wife of a Piedmont banker who is also a very dedicated Christian, will lead a women's organization at the chapel. At first it was thought this meeting should be on Friday, but Mrs. Everett decided on Monday at 2 p.m. All the other women from Piedmont Wesleyan Methodist have agreed, it seems, to support this program, as well as other activities of the mission.

Some of these activities will be: an athletic program of softball, basketball etc., a club for boys which will probably be led by Mr. Grant, and one of the ladies has agreed to conduct a girls' club. Some of these members may lead the midweek evening service when Rev. Durham does not do it.

Rev. Durham says Mr. Catlett, who is the proprietor of Catlett Wholesale Grocery Co., will be director of the Sunday school at the chapel until it is well started. Most of the men coming into the mission from Piedmont Wesleyan Methodist will serve as a board of stewards for the chapel. Mr. Morton, who is a lawyer, Mr. Beaver and Mr. Grant are currently members of the board at the mother church.

Would this do? It would not. The order is wrong. The account is wordy at some points with occasional editorializing (need for the mission, wonderful ministry, very dedicated Christians). Titles are incorrectly used (Rev. Durham), first-mentioned names incomplete, identifications erratic. There is quite a bit of extraneous material, even some guesswork.

Four

It Take All Kinds

A list of the types of material suitable for news stories would be almost endless. When we finally got it made out something would pop up which could be fitted into none of the categories. Anyway it might be useful to indicate a few of the types of stories you will need to deal with in religion news writing.

Simple announcements. Here the objective is to give essential facts in the shortest space possible. If the time of meeting for the Sunday evening worship service has been changed from 7:30 to 8:00 o'clock, state this, giving name and location of the church, along with the source of information perhaps, and the job is done.

If some event or decision is being reported and its significance is small, content yourself with a brief notice. Normal changes of pastorate would be of this type, except for outstanding leaders and churches, unless the news is for a small-town paper. Many deaths would be reported in the same brief way (see section on obituaries), as well as most births. Don't claim space for a long story if there is no call for it.

Achievement. If the pastor who is changing his place of work has made an outstanding record in his previous pastorate, by all means make a full story of it. If it lasted several decades, this in itself is news. How does the membership as he leaves compare in size and activity with when he came? Has he led in the erection of new buildings? Has he occupied positions of responsibility in denominational, interdenominational or civic organizations? Does he give particular reasons for leaving? Any pertinent remarks from him would be of interest, as well as comments about him from members of the congregation or of the one to which he is going.

Don't forget that lay people achieve things too. Report who won the Bible-usage or other contests in your district or state and tell something about their church life, ways of training for the contest, daily work and other points of interest concerning the competition.

Group achievement is noteworthy. If "people are news," an accomplishment involving many people may likely be of greater interest than one in which few were concerned. Which church led the denomination in baptisms or in gifts? What Sunday schools had the highest attendance? Do some of the churches have outstanding choirs, orchestras, handbell groups, drama clubs, ball teams? Any of this means news, but it is not always reported.

Anniversaries. This is a perennially favorite type of story, both in the secular and religious press. It includes not only commemoration of births and deaths of church fathers but anniversaries of pastorates, service as deacons, stewards, elders, Sunday school teachers, youth leaders, caretakers and cooks.

Anniversaries in round numbers such as 10th, 25th, 50th and 100th are best. You must consider the extent in time and the importance or interest in general attached to the person or group commemorated and decide whether it is newsworthy. If it is, call attention to the anniversary date, give some background and write up the story around interesting facts in connection with the memorable occasion.

Elections. All churches have some kind of organization, as do various groups within them. There are national and district unions and interdenominational Christian movements. These organizations have officers and committees that must be elected or appointed from time to time. Not all of this is news but much of it definitely is.

Your story about an election should treat most prominently one or two leading officers that have been chosen. Minor ones can be omitted or listed at the end. Be sure to put some meat on the bones of the report. Tell something of the previous work of new officers, the job they are undertaking and their outlook in the new position.

Decisions. Conclusions reached by various church bodies are news, as are those by individual leaders which affect the work. This may mean a report on some official's sudden decision to resign. In such an event the "why" might be the prominent element of the story. Also the "how" as to what is to be done to meet the emergency, if any, resulting from the resignation.

Speech. If someone is going to make a speech that you think will justify a news story, be there to hear it. Editors of the city dailies sometimes depend on telephone reports for their religion speech stories, but this is because they do not consider them important enough to send someone from their limited staff of reporters to cover them.

Get a copy of the speech in advance if possible. Even if you succeed in this, don't sleep while the address is in progress. The speaker may change something.

Be sure you know what the purpose of the meeting is, who is sponsoring it, name and identification of the presiding officer as well as the speaker.

Notice the speaker when he appears. Pay attention to his appearance and manner as well as his words. Observe the audience too. Study their reaction at crucial points. It may well be that these various observations will be as important for your story as the content of the speech itself.

Be on the lookout for the unexpected. Maybe your story will eventually center around that. Don't be like the cub reporter who, it is said, returned shamefacedly to his editor saying it was impossible to do a good story on the speaker he had been sent to cover. Somebody had shot him before he was halfway through the address!

In case you are without a copy of the speaker's manuscript, don't try to take down everything, even if you master a good system of shorthand. You will not be able to observe well if you do, and you must spend a lot of time later translating your shorthand notes, or transcribing the speech if you taped it on a recorder. All this is quite unecessary.

Try to follow the speaker's general train of thought and get down a few crucial sentences exactly as delivered. These direct quotations improve your story. You could use up to a third or even half within quotation marks, with the remainder consisting of indirect quotation, summary, background and description. Alternate quoted material with the other.

If you are uncertain about the exactness of quotations, check with the speaker if possible after the meeting. Be sure to get all names spelled exactly right, with identifications in proper form.

Meeting. This is an extension of the speech story. The meeting probably includes more than one speaker, however, and there may be business of importance that is attended to.

You have to decide which speaker or business to feature and start with that, unless you list several points in series as your opening.

Here as elsewhere be aware of your responsibility as a reporter. You want to make your story interesting and naturally you will feature striking remarks or decisions, but be careful not to leave the impression that these were the important and representative things unless they really were. You have an obligation to the people involved, yourself, your paper and its readers to be fair. This does not mean to be dull.

Convention. This is a further extension of the above. The convention or conference—whether district, national or international—will have numerous speakers and likely much business also. Your task is a bit more difficult here, if your assignment or undertaking is to do the "wrap up" story on the gathering as a whole.

You will have to be even more determined in omitting items, perhaps even that most profound speech of all. You must select something to give main attention to, then list several others briefly.

You might want to start with a quotation from the keynote speaker, give a further sentence or two concerning his address. This could be followed with important facts about the convention or conference and some of the votes taken, then something from one or two other speeches. The new slate of officers or the time and place of the next such assembly might conclude the story.

Obituary. This should probably begin with full name and brief identification of the deceased, age, occupation, residence and possibly the mention of connection with some well known person. It may be mentioned that he or she died unexpectedly or after a long illness, and frequently the cause of death is given.

This would normally be followed by details of his or her career, birthplace, church and other affiliations, positions held.

Survivors in the immediate family are usually listed, with place of residence and possibly further identification. In a daily-paper obituary published immediately after the death, time and place of funeral are given, along with mention of officiating minister and funeral directors.

Other types. There are other kinds of news stories that are prominent in the daily press but seldom appear in religion journalism. Crime stories fortunately do not often feature people who are newsworthy in the field of religion.

Disaster stories do need attention from time to time in this field of journalism. The rule here is that people are more important than things. People killed or injured, unless injury is slight, are mentioned before property damage. Both should be included, however, along with explanation of just what happened, how and why.

Five

Interviews And Biography

Most of the news that appears in the daily papers comes from interviews somewhere; these are conducted either in person or by telephone as a rule. Religion papers would gain in accuracy and vitality by relating themselves more directly with subjects through numerous interviews. Usually there is not the reportorial staff for it. Here again is the opportunity waiting with open arms for you in free-lance religion writing.

A hearsay report from a member about the building of a new addition to some church may need to be checked by interviews with the pastor, the chairman of the building committee and the contractor.

If you hear that an evangelistic campaign is being planned in a certain neighborhood, you will want to find out from the host pastor about the program and leaders, then contact the evangelist and musicians if possible. Talk with some members of the church also, if you want a complete story.

In such cases people are interviewed simply because they are sources for news about certain events and plans.

In some stories, however, a particular person is the subject. If a leading theologian or youth leader is visiting your town, interview him for a story about his views and his work. To make it more than a superficial reporting of just what the person happened to have on his mind that day, you may describe him or her and give something of the background and present situation. Then you will have a news feature or perhaps a personality sketch. For a thorough job on this more than one interview may be necessary.

It is not only the prominent person who makes a good subject for an interview. It may be a typical one, such as the postman, pastor or policeman. It might be someone who has a very unusual hobby or profession, or one of long experience in a particular field of work.

How do you get the interview? Usually for ordinary people there is no difficulty about this, except arranging the time. They are happy to talk with you and honored by your wishing to write about them.

With particularly busy and prominent persons it can be a problem. You must try to convince your subject that it is worthwhile for him and for the cause you may both be interested in.

Be careful not to promise too much. Do not let your subject believe that you will manipulate the material to put him in a favorable light, or that you will avoid mentioning any weakness.

For one who has been accused of unworthy activity of some sort, or who may expect that the reporter will be critical, there might be outright refusal to grant the interview. If you are faced with such a situation and consider it important to get the story, you may persist by explaining that it will be better for the public to have the facts straight than through distorted reports and rumors that are going around.

You do not want to boast, but it is not a bad idea to let your subject know that you are able to do the job in a responsible way. Unless this is your very first such interview, you might casually mention some others you have done.

If you have an assignment, or even if the editor of a paper has just agreed to accept the story on speculation, you may mention to the subject that you are writing it for that publication with which you have had contact. Even if you haven't approached the editor beforehand, you can still say you will submit the piece to a certain newspaper or periodical.

This will help to reassure your subject that you are not an irresponsible amateur whose writings are unlikely to get beyond his notebook, and the subject will more readily give the needed time and cooperation.

You should inform yourself as well as you can about the subject before appearing for the interview. If books or articles have been written by or about the person, read these if possible. You may want to speak with some of his or her friends, even associates who are not friendly, before or following the interview.

Make a list of questions calculated to stimulate interesting comments. Keep your prospective readers in mind as you decide on topics to be brought up. What would *they* like to know about this person, his ideas, life and work if they had the opportunity as you do of speaking with him or her?

What the particular questions should be depends on each individual case, but here are some things to keep in mind. Consider the interviewee's daily work, avocations and other interests, background, turning points in life, influential persons, problems, attitudes, unfulfilled ambitions, achievements and goals.

How does he or she feel about the daily job, associates, prospects? A voracious reader, active in sports, a zealous patriot? What special ideas in the field of principal interest? Does the subject have particular complaints or suggestions regarding whatever it is he or she is involved in?

Find out about the interviewee's family. Don't forget to consider the feelings as well as important events in the subject's life. Observe personal appearance, characteristic movements, mannerisms and idiosyncracies, whether likeable or objectionable.

Remember the words of Plutarch, Greek biographer and moralist of about A.D. 100: "An action of a small note, a short saying or a jest distinguishes a person's character more than the greatest sieges or most important battles."

Should you take notes at the interview or use a tape recorder? Some say neither, particularly if you have a subject who seems to be made uncomfortable by the idea that what he says is being frozen into literature before his very eyes. Just have an informal conversation (one that appears to be unplanned but is not) and dash away afterward to write down what you can remember. But unless you have a phenomenal memory or forego direct quotes, this method will not work very well. Use it only if you have to.

A small tape recorder would seem to be the best solution, unless the subject objects. Don't use it secretly but turn it on unobtrusively and place it matter-of-factly before the two of you somewhat as if you were laying down some small purchase from previous shopping just to free your hands for talk!

Use of the recorder to get the interview down is indeed a good method, *if* the contraption works! In case you have an economical model as I do (a really good one costs hundreds), you probably won't have much faith in it and checking it out all along is a considerable distraction to both you and your subject. Also, replaying the tape repeatedly as you work afterward with it, or having it transcribed, will be costly in time and maybe money.

I'd say, use the tape recorder but don't depend on it. Just refer to it later to get down exactly those parts you use as direct quotation. Take some notes anyway.

If you have reason to fear that even this will disturb your subject, making him too stilted and reserved in his replies to your questions, you might make a point of asking, near the beginning of the conversation, place and date of birth and exact spelling of names (which you probably know already). Then take out paper and pencil saying you want to jot that down to be sure you have it just right. Perhaps the subject will take this as a matter of course and hardly give it another thought as you take further notes also from time to time.

One reporter as he goes to interviews makes a habit of carrying a newspaper under his arm, folded so that an advertisement with lots of white space is on top. He drops the paper in a natural way on his knee as he sits down, and likely as not the paper is hidden from the subject's view by the latter's desk. The reporter makes most of his notes without looking down.

Another interviewer says he carries a pad of paper in his coat pocket and scribbles notes on it there. In a variation of this plan, still another declares he has a pencil lead attached to his ring for pocket writing. You and I had better not depend on such methods!

Many people, especially those accustomed to being interviewed, have a feeling of confidence when they observe that care is being taken to get down in correct form exactly what they say, whether this be in writing or on a cassette recorder. Their fear of being misquoted is allayed.

If you want a system of shorthand for your notetaking and don't know one, you can work it out on your own. Begin by ignoring most vowels and many consonants. For each frequently used word select a single letter or two. B can stand for Bible, C or X for Christ, J for Jesus, Cn or Xn for Christian, Cy or Xy for Christianity, ch for church, Jn for John, t (made and crossed in one stroke)that, ti this, Am America, ab about, q question, O nothing and so on. Use letters and numbers for the names of them: b for be, 2b for to be, b4 for before, c for see and sea as well as circa etc.

Add to your shorthand vocabulary by studying the abbreviations section in the unabridged dictionary; decide on symbols and combinations for your own particular needs.

Spell out names in full, except for the most common, and all rarely used words so that accuracy will not be jeopardized. Forms of the verb "to be" and other minor words may often be omitted in your note taking, but beware of abbreviating beyond the competent reach of your system. Do not sacrifice accuracy for speed, not even out of consideration for the feelings of a shy subject. Ask him or her to slow down, if you have to, in order for you to get down what you want.

If the interviewee indicates that certain remarks are "off the record," you may be faced with a problem. One way is just to stop him when he starts a sentence like "This is not for publication, but . . . ." You may prefer to tell the subject that you'd rather not hear anything you are not free to use. On the topic in question, if it is important to your purpose, you might be able to get the information elsewhere.

On the other hand, you may wish to have your subject speak as freely as he or she will, in order to get background knowledge, then try to convince the person that it is to the best interest of all concerned that permission be granted for the use of those points that are important to your purpose.

Ordinarily, with the subjects you face as a free lance religion writer, there will probably be little difficulty not only in getting interviews but also in quoting statements made. The people with whom you deal may protest that their story is not worth telling, but if the interview is agreed to, they will likely be cooperative, appreciative of your interest in them and their work.

Even if you have complete notes and a tape recording, don't wait any longer than necessary to write up the piece, the first draft anyway. It will surely be more vivid and interesting if you do it right away. Many subtle but significant points, particularly in regard to the appearance and characteristics of your subject, may not come to mind at all or remain hazy if you wait days or weeks to begin the writing.

Go through all of your material, arrange and rearrange until you have worked out a satisfactory organization for the article. Often you will want to begin with an interesting anecdote that dramatically and fairly represents an important part of your subject's way of life. Sometimes a striking statement or quotation is the best beginning. Occasionally the news type summary lead may suit.

A more informal approach is to describe the subject as you saw him or her in office or home, then to relate something of the conversation and describe your impressions. Don't forget to include comments of other people about your subject if these help to fill in the picture.

In the personality sketch or "profile," which we have

been considering, you must not feel bound to the chronological order. You may eventually decide to follow through in this order, after an introductory anecdote chosen from a later period, but probably not. In this type of biographical piece, especially if it is a brief personality sketch, you may be close to the end of the article before you get around to mentioning the subject's background, time and place of birth and so on.

Be sure to save something effective with which to finish the sketch. This may be a quotation from the subject which seems to epitomize his life and work, a remark of someone else about the person, a summary or your own final estimate. It may be an anecdote which sums up what you have to say about the subject and brings the piece to an honest and satisfying conclusion.

Should you submit the finished manuscript to the subject for approval? If you have treated controversial issues, this might be a good idea as protection for you. Some reporters in such cases get the subject to sign the copy as factually correct. He or she should be made to understand that this does not bind the reporter to get the thing published in exactly that form; primarily it just attests to the accuracy of direct quotations.

Ordinarily such precautions are unecessary. And you may just be asking for trouble if you submit your manuscript to the subject, especially to one who is unaccustomed to such things. He or she may be assailed by doubt as to the advisability of allowing any of the more interesting details to be published. He may raise objection to the most innocuous criticisms or allusions. Use of the story could be delayed indefinitely while the subject makes up his mind, or what remains after his deletions may be useless.

Speedy submission for publication, after careful and responsible "censorship" by you the writer, is probably in most cases best. You should get a copy of the printed article to your subject as soon as possible and seeing this will likely show him or her that there was nothing to fear from it. The person will probably be delighted with the publicity received.

One interviewer reads his article over the telephone to his subject, asking if the quotes and facts are correct, and approval is granted forthwith almost without exception. If this is done soon after the interview and the writing fairly represents it, the subject gets the general impression that it is all right. Hearing it read in this way, with emphasis given in the proper places, the subject will not pay so much attention to minor points that might otherwise stand out as question marks and possible threats to his or her reputation from seeing the manuscript. This is not a bad system.

If you are writing a formal biographical article, such as for a learned journal, your approach will be more objective. Your sources will be indicated in footnotes and bibliography. You will be more likely to follow the chronological or a strictly topical order. Paragraphs and sentences might be longer. Technical or jargon words would be allowable if they really carry more weight for your intelligent readers than simple and popular words. Anecdotes may be less in evidence, while ideas are treated in depth.

There are of course periodicals that like material in between this and the personality profile for the popular market. Always study carefully the publications you write for and fit your method to the opportunity.

Live subjects are the best, other things being equal, but not at all the only source of material for biographical pieces. Reducing the full length biography (or several of them on the same subject) concerning some interesting person in history to a thousand words or less may be the best way to start in the wonderful world of writing, especially for the timid beginner. Almost every kind of periodical and newspaper would like to have more biographical material if subjects are well chosen and appropriately treated.

Be sure to read at least one standard biography on your historical subject and some additional material if available. He or she may have been an outstanding church leader, missionary or crusader for some good cause.

Pick out the important and interesting points in his or her career, choose suitable experiences to relate and dramatize the piece. You had better leave out personal evaluations in your first efforts, omit the moralizing and pious remarks both first and thereafter, let your subject reveal himself or herself in what is said and done.

Biographical writing is one of the most popular forms, especially in religion. The field is so vast that you will surely find plenty of subjects and markets that are suited to your interest and talents.

Here is a short biographical piece I sold many years ago to *Upward*, a Sunday school weekly for young people published at that time in Nashville, Tennessee:

Explanation of a Life

Bill Borden had a problem: he was rich. Bill's father, related to developers of the Borden milk concern, died in 1906 when Bill was a freshman at Yale University, leaving the boy largely in control of the family fortune.

This constituted an invitation to a life of luxury and idleness. If Bill Borden ever considered adopting such a life style, no one ever saw signs of it. He worked hard and lived as thriftily as he could.

His mother was an especially devoted Christian, active in a conservative Chicago church, and Bill was converted at an early age.

He felt the money was not his but God's. No one knows how much he gave away, but check stubs from the latter part of his college career show more than $70,000 donated to religious work and charity. His will divided the fortune, after his death, among various religious agencies.

One day Bill Borden was standing on a street corner with a friend when a new automobile sped by; motor cars were still rather a novelty at the time.

"How I'd like to have one," Bill said longingly. He never did buy an auto, although he could have had hundreds, because he did not feel he really needed it.

Simply devoting money was not enough for Bill. He gave much of his time to YMCA and other religious activities on and off campus. He helped organize Yale Hope Mission on the New Haven waterfront. He was an enthusiastic personal worker at the mission and among his fellow students.

"Why, the way he came amongst us," one of the men who attended the mission for help related later, "you would never think he was a man of wealth, and he always dressed so plain . . . "

"It couldn't seem possible a man could be so humble and yet so great. He could talk to anyone, didn't matter who they was; and he'd get down with his arms around the poor burly bum and hug him up.

"I know he must have done for hundreds just what he done for me," the man said. "He was always trying to study into the lives of men, to see how they'd work out and how he could help 'em."

Bill had been given a trip around the world upon his graduation from high school. While traveling in the Far East he began to feel that perhaps he should devote his life to missionary service.

It was at a Student Volunteer convention in Nashville, to which he had gone as a delegate from Yale, that he made the full commitment. This came at the conclusion of an appeal by Samuel Zwemer, missionary to Muslim lands. Bill Borden resolved to serve among the neglected Muslims of China.

Upon graduation from Princeton Seminary, he accepted an appointment to his chosen field under the China Inland Mission. The plan was for him to spend a year in Cairo studying the life and classical language of Muslim peoples. Dr. Zwemer was there and would assist him in making the most of his preparation.

Young Borden was having a great time in this center of Islam. He enjoyed his study of Arabic language and culture, delighted in fellowship with missionaries in Cairo.

It is not surprising to learn that he also began, on his own, a friendly work among the nationals; many of these became devoted to him. He left the hotel and went to live in an Egyptian home, was often mistaken for a national as he moved naturally among them.

Borden had always enjoyed

perfect health. He had been active in college athletics—baseball, wrestling, football, boat-racing—and continued afterward to keep himself in good physical condition.

Suddenly now, without any kind of warning, he was stricken with cerebral meningitis. After nineteen days of uncertainty he died quietly in April 1913, four hours before his mother and sister could reach his bedside.

He was only twenty-five and had not yet reached his chosen field for life's labor, but surely William Borden lived a more complete life than many who reach old age.

When I was in Cairo some time ago I was more anxious to visit Borden's grave than I was to see the pyramids. His life inspired me as it did many others of my student generation.

The Egyptian caretaker of the cemetery recognized at once the name of "Mister Borden," although he spoke little or no English. He kindly took my wife and me to the quiet, shady corner of the cemetery where the grave was located.

The stone was not elaborate, but its inscription put into one sentence the final word, I think, in any true estimate of William Borden: "Apart from faith in Christ there is no explanation for such a life."

Six

The General Feature Article

Although newspapers and magazines show no signs of being displaced by radio and television, their character and role have changed somewhat. You have heard of papers and magazines that have been crushed to the wall by the relentless laws of our economy. It seems that publishing a newspaper is so expensive now that only the fittest survive, and some large cities no longer have really competitive dailies. But readership has not declined, I feel sure, and magazines flourish in large numbers.

One adjustment in the role of newspapers is that they give more space to interpretive reporting, comics, columns by commentators and general feature stories.

The broadcaster reports spot news more quickly than it can be printed and distributed by newspapers. He generally has time for little else, however, and often the small bit of information given about an interesting event only whets the listener's appetite to know more. He counts on finding it in his newspaper and newsmagazines.

Feature stories, especially those for the daily press, often have a news peg, that is, some obvious point at which they are related to events being reported in the news. They supplement news stories by reporting in depth, giving background information, presenting outstanding personalities who are involved and describing places connected with events in the news.

Besides these feature articles directly related to the news, others deal with topics of perennial interest. Questions of health, self-improvement, family life, ways to do interesting or useful things, success stories, topics of interest to older citizens or other large groups of the population, tax problems, investment opportunities and travel fall into this class. A subject of interest to readers, for whatever reason, is grist for the feature writer's mill.

It is not only in newspapers and religious journals that the religion writer can find markets for his feature articles, but also in the vast field of general periodical publications. Many of these may rarely if ever print features about religion, but this is often due to the fact that they get so few that are up to their standards and prepared in a form readily understood and appreciated by their readers.

The most important thing to remember about the feature article is that it deals with facts, or at least with what you as the writer sincerely believe, after careful investigation, to be factual. Facts are the life blood of the feature story, and it should be packed with them.

Be careful in research, whether this be mainly in books or in talks with people and personal observation, to be sure you have all the pertinent facts straight. The quickest way to get on the blacklist of any editor is to be careless in this. The editor will not soon forget his embarrassment, or worse, on printing something you sent in which turned out to be not exactly right.

An encyclopedia article deals with facts too, but it differs vastly from a good feature story written for a newspaper or periodical. What is the difference? Just this: the feature gets the facts to the reader painlessly, even entertainingly, and probably deals with people more. It should be written in such a way that the average reader of that particular publication can sail through it, with understanding and enjoyment, as readily as in reading his favorite fiction.

How do you decide on a subject? See the next chapter for some suggestions, which are just to get you started on a list of your own. The main trouble in this field of writing is not to find a good subject but to choose from among thousands, almost any of which are good if you will only work them up.

When your subject is in a field well known to you, there may be enough material in your own experience and knowledge to deal with it. Usually, however, you will need to refer to familiar sources at least, review recent developments or speak with knowledgeable people about it.

Some writers like to specialize, dealing almost exclusively with youth work or evangelism, for example, literacy movements or mission. There are plenty of opportunities to make this possible, and then each project is somewhat familiar to you from the start. Many writers are bored by such a regimen, however, preferring to delve into a new subject every few weeks. Certainly this gives spice and variety to the writer's life.

You do not have to be a specialist in a field in order to report work being done in it. Some feel it is even better for the writer to be a layman in the field. It is easy for him in this case to place himself in his readers' shoes and avoid technical jargon. He remembers to explain things which might be assumed by the specialist to be common knowledge but are not.

Even when the field is new to you, you must make yourself a sort of temporary specialist. Visit the library, if this is what seems to be called for, and read in any event what you can find about the subject you are working on.

Don't forget files in the periodical section. With the riches of a good library available, it has been said, the writer can make himself the second best informed person on any subject, next to the one who wrote the best books on it!

You must be the judge as to when you have read enough. Naturally you cannot cover everything if it is a broad subject, or you will never get around to setting pen to paper. It is usually better to choose limited subjects, and maybe those on which you can get most of your material from life rather than printed sources.

As you begin to organize the materials you have gathered, do not assume, here again, that the order should be chronological, even with historical articles. Choose the most effective arrangement. Don't try to work all your notes into the article. Cold-bloodedly omit even seemingly important parts, or really good anecdotes, if they do not contribute to your purpose.

Like an iceberg, only a small part of your work may appear on the surface, but the unseen part will have been almost as important as that which comes to the light of day. If the final writing includes all you know on the subject, this will be fatally evident. Readers like to feel that the author is sharing that which is most important and interesting from his large reservoir of knowledge in the field.

As with the biographical piece, you will often start off the general feature with a striking anecdote or statement, quotation or description, rarely perhaps a summary lead as in the news story.

The beginning must grab the interest of your reader, and the rest of the story should hold him securely. Save some interesting incident or statement for the ending. Remember, the reader can stop any time he wants to, and he probably will if you do not write with his concerns in mind.

You may even "plot" the article somewhat like a short story, attracting your reader, getting him involved and making him willing to wait for the end to see how you will wind up the story.

Usually you will desire some particular effect on your reader. You might in some cases suggest outright what needs to be done and what part readers should undertake. More often, your purpose will be more modest and your method more subtle, involving perhaps only a slight change in the reader's ideas or point of view, or just furnishing some entertainment and useful information.

Almost all feature stories need illustrations, photographic or otherwise. You can purchase photographs from suppliers listed in writers' market books, but it will be much cheaper and more satisfactory in most cases for you to get some good simple equipment and take your own pictures. Follow instructions, avoid tricky angles and results will probably be satisfactory for most journalistic purposes. Free photographs may sometimes be secured from chambers of commerce, airlines, church agencies and consulates of foreign countries.

For many articles you will have a much better chance of placing them if they are accompanied by large glossy prints (eight by ten inches or at least five by seven). Pencil a number lightly on the back of each photo, then type a list of brief descriptions according to the numbers. You just might be paid as much for the illustrations as for the article.

My first sale was to the Methodist youth paper, *Classmate*, Nashville, Tennessee, and it was published March 31, 1946:

The Mountain That Blew Its Top

It was one of those trips you are glad you made but never would have if you had known in advance what it involved.

We were told at the Serviceman's Red Cross that the Vesuvius trip required an hour of hard climbing and was bad on the shoes. But things like that just don't seem to sink in until it's too late. In any case it was a marvel of understatement. It's just as well, though; I'm glad I went, now that it's over.

My wife Pauline and I, along with seven others, took the train at Naples (Italy) station for Publiano, which is ten miles southeast of the city. There we boarded a funicular railway car, which took us part way up the mountain.

The lower slopes of Vesuvius are covered with grass, shrubs and small trees. The lava, after being pulverized for a few centuries, makes a fertile soil. Farther up, fairly recent eruptions have left black barrenness.

In the time of Christ the higher slopes and even the plateau at the top were covered with green meadows and tilled fields, we were told. In the year A.D. 63 earthquakes began there, followed by a series of eruptions, climaxing with the great explosion of A.D. 79 which sent out rivers of boiling lava to destroy every living thing within its reach.

It was at this time that Pompeii was destroyed. Even though lava did not reach the city, it was buried under countless tons of hot ashes.

There have been hundreds of eruptions since then, sometimes several in a year. During other periods the volcano remained quiet for many years. The eruption of 1636, just to take an example, destroyed five towns and killed many people; but the volcano had been apparently dead for nearly a century and a half before that. Vegetation grew all over it and cattle grazed in the crater.

Until the most recent eruption, in the spring of 1944, Vesuvius mountain was rather cone-shaped at the top. That explosion was so violent, however, that the head of the mountain was blown off. The rim at the top is now four hundred feet lower than the crest was before and the cavity in the center much deeper.

When we had gone about half way up the side of the mountain, we arrived at a great pile of lava left by the 1944 eruption, and the funicular car came to a stop. The obstacle looked like a heap of coal thirty or forty feet high extending like a crude wall to our right and left around that side of the mountain, along a slight depression.

The funicular rails, before they disappeared under the black mass, twisted outward several feet. Our guide told us this had been caused by the 2,200 degree Fahrenheit heat of boiling lava.

Nearby there was a small building of cement and stone, whose steel girders had been burned away at their edges by the heat. Charred lava was heaped up against the walls of this building, but it held and is still being used as a funicular maintenance station.

We walked over the hill of lava and took a smaller cog-driven car. It was puzzling to us how the cars happened to be on that side of the lava mass. The guide grinned and said, "The American army did that."

The army engineers had transferred a few of the cars across the lava hill so that an hour of hard climbing is saved for the sightseer. We rode in the little car up to a point where the tracks disappeared again, this time for good.

From there we set out for the hard climb over sharp lava rocks and cinders. It took at least an hour and a quarter of steady climbing. Pauline and I thought many times that we just couldn't make it. Two of the American soldiers who were with us did turn back.

To start with it wasn't too bad. At least there was a path. One had of course to watch his step over the sharp black rocks, some of which were not secure. It was more difficult when the path became a narrow ledge along the side of a steep slope. We would have been grateful for that, however, if we had known what lay ahead.

The latter half of the hike took us up a steep path incline to the crest. It was difficult to find the "path" and if you did, it was more of the same. Just imagine trying to climb a mountain of ashes and cinders with soft pebbles and sharp rocks thrown in. We would step up a couple of feet and slide back one or more as cinders gave way underfoot. The closer we got to the top the tougher the going became.

Occasionally there was a large stone and we took advantage of each one to sit down and rest. This could be only for a moment, however. Our sixty-five year old guide pressed steadily onward and upward. When we rested we'd have to hurry then to catch up. That old guide makes the trip twice a day.

Finally we reached the top, painfully exhausted. What met our eyes was a sight that took our breath away, if we had any left. We were standing on the edge of a huge cup, almost a quarter of a mile across and approximately that deep.

Our guide said we were lucky to be there while the crater was smoking—unusual during the past year. While we were standing there on the rim watching smoke ooze from a crack on the opposite side of the crater, a more unusual thing occured.

From the same spot there began a series of explosions with loud crackling noises; smoke and dust belched out until they filled the crater. Pauline insisted that we leave, and we did. We didn't want to wait for anything *too* unusual to happen!

The descent was faster but just as difficult, even more destructive to our shoes. We would take a step, let the foot sink into the ashes and slide a foot or two, then repeat the operation with the other foot. It didn't happen as slowly as it sounds. It was impossible to walk; we were obliged to run. With a long step and a long slide each time, we were moving with great giant strides.

The outer leather of my shoes was ripped to shreds. Pauline had skin torn from her heels. We were both aching and exhausted. We made it back to the first funicular car, however, and collapsed thankfully on its board seats.

Before the 1944 eruption tourists were able to ride to the top. I wonder whether they realized how fortunate they were! The official tourist agency is already working on plans to reconstruct the entire funicular line. I want to go back, when they do—but not before!

Seven

An ABC Of Feature Ideas

Advertising. What churches in your area use paid advertisements in newspapers to announce services? Ask ministers and others whether they consider them effective. Give examples of results. What information is given in the announcements? Is there a picture of the pastor or the church? What about cost? Is more space taken for special meetings? Which churches have a special listing in the yellow pages of the telephone directory? Have any ever bought space for publishing brief devotional or evangelistic messages in the newspapers?

What is the extent of advertising in church papers? How do rates compare with secular papers of comparable circulation? What types of advertisers would not be accepted in the church papers? Is there objection to advertising which has been used? Are substantial discounts given to churches and agencies such as children's and retirement homes, colleges and publishing departments of the same denomination? What about other denominations and nondenominational agencies?

Other article ideas in regard to individual churches: Do they have notice boards in front of the buildings? Give examples of the types of material that are posted— announcements, personnel, mottoes, epigrams etc. How often is the message changed? Ask some members and others their impressions. Were some first attracted to the church by its bulletin board?

Are placards posted or handbills distributed to advertise special church events? Are there spot advertising announcements and other programs on radio and TV?

Answers to questions in each of the above paragraphs, along with other questions that will occur to you, can provide material for an article or a series of articles.

Adult Education. Do some of the churches have evening school or classes for adults or senior adults not only in religious education or doctrine but perhaps in literacy training, public speaking, archeology, languages, art or music as well? Are extension courses from some college or theological seminary offered? Interview teachers and participants. What do local or nearby colleges offer in evening schools or in their day classes? Are discounts offered for senior citizens?

Airplanes. Interview evangelists and other religious workers who use private planes in their work, or get in touch with foreign missionaries on furlough (or write to them) who use small planes in their work. Describe the Pilots' Club at a seminary in California that has a training program for interested students, or that of any other such institution you can find. Tell about outstanding pilots who were also outstanding Christians such as Captain Mitsuo Fuchida, who led the Japanese attack on Pearl Harbor in 1941 and was later converted, or Jim Erwin, astronaut who landed on the moon and later established an evangelistic agency.

Archeology. Do archeological discoveries generally substantiate biblical accuracy? What light is thrown on the ways of life in ancient times by the unearthing of former civilizations? Give examples of present-day benefits from such knowledge. Interview one or more persons who have taken part in archeological work.

Architecture. What are the main trends in church and/or temple architecture today? What differences are there in various countries and religious groups? Describe some imaginative and striking designs; illustrate with photographs. Give the reactions of members, lay and clerical, to "modern" architecture. Interview architects who have built outstanding churches, temples or synagogues. Consider the influence of traditional forms of religious architecture through the centuries.

Art. How much of the great art of the world has been produced in connection with religious faith and practice? Focus this in regard to Christianity of the Western world, the U.S. or your own area. Compare art being produced today with that of past centuries. Consider the murals in St. Peter's of Rome and other famous churches, also individual paintings by great artists with religious themes. What paintings are regarded as the greatest, the most valuable? Which are your favorites? Why? Describe local galleries and give examples of their paintings. Other articles can deal with other types of art.

Baptistries and baptismal fonts. Describe the most general types in various religious groups, also some of the most extreme. Describe baptismal services including spoken parts, administrator, subject, dress and manner of conducting the rite. Mention some unusual happenings in connection with baptisms. Do some groups reject man-made baptistries in favor of running streams? Research ancient baptistries in buildings separate from the church etc. Does the structure of the oldest baptistries indicate a particular mode of baptism? What was the ancient order of service; when and why changed?

Born again. This term has come into national prominence by our having a confessed "born again" U.S. president, Jimmy Carter. Mention other outstanding persons who use the term. Consider its biblical background, history. Give some illustrative anecdotes. What church groups emphasize it most? Approximately what part of the U.S. population would claim a born-again experience? Apply estimates locally, if this would seem to be in good taste and it is for a newspaper; and give some local quotes.

Bazaars. How prevalent are religion-sponsored bazaars today and how different are they from those held in earlier times? Give colorful examples. Are most of the items that are put on sale made by members of the congregation, or purchased and then donated? Are biblical objections raised to the holding of bazaars? What effect, if any, does it seem that bazaars have on giving or in general? Indicate the most successful methods used by those that hold bazaars.

Bible. Start perhaps with the story of someone whose life was dramatically changed by reading the Bible. What are the views of church leaders and others as to the authority of the Bible? When and where did the collection of books now in the "Protestant" (or the Catholic) Bible come to be accepted as the canon of scripture? Consider various versions, Bible societies, preservation in times of persecution or in Siberian labor camps today and the number of languages into which the Bible has been translated. Give attitudes toward the Bible by some outstanding non-Christians as well as church leaders. In what ways do Mormons, Christian Scientists and Jews make use of the Bible?

Books. Estimate the number printed in the world and in the U.S. during the past year, after checking the best sources available. What proportion of those published in this country were in the field of religion? Name the current "best sellers" of this group. Compare the relative popularity of fiction and fact books. Describe the work of some religion writers, past and present. Do additional articles in various divisions of this vast field.

Budgets. Contrast congregations with million-dollar annual budgets and others with budgets of a few thousand or no budget at all. What items are included in such budgets, and what proportions for the main categories? Who works out the budget? Must it be approved by the entire membership? Are pledges taken and, if so, are most of them paid?

Buses. What experiences have local or other churches had in busing children and older people to Sunday school and worship services? Does the church own buses, or vans? Do church leaders feel the program has been successful, that those transported in this way would for the most part not have come otherwise, that overall attendence has increased because of it? Who are the bus drivers? Tell some interesting experiences they have had. Do they receive remuneration, or special recognition such as in the action of one church in Florida that ordained its "bus deacons."

Another article might result from interviews with ministers or others who customarily travel by Greyhound or Continental Trailways. Relate some of their interesting and unusual contacts while riding the buses and their general impressions. Get them to estimate their total bus mileage. What do they consider the advantages and disadvantages of bus travel?

Interviews with Christian bus drivers of long experience would also provide interesting material for an article.

Business. Do religious institutions have good business ratings as a rule? Inquire of those who compile such ratings, why this is so or not. Do many churches have paid business administrators? What are their duties? Are these churches judged to be using funds and conducting their work more efficiently? Should laymen be encouraged to help apply methods used in the business world to make church work more efficient? Should more money be invested in modern business equipment and in efficiency surveys? How do ministers rate in business judgment and administration?

Specifically in bookkeeping, do religious organizations as a rule keep good financial records? Quote the opinions of businessmen. Tell of occurrences where money was saved or lost, disaster hastened or avoided by care in keeping books carefully. Do many churches have paid bookkeepers? What are the main principles for amateurs who do this work to keep in mind? Is equipment and training costly, compared with the need for better bookkeeping?

Carnival. Although not now generally associated with religion, the word is from Latin terms signifying to "put away flesh" or "good-bye, flesh." Originally it was the period preceding Lent. This season of feasting and joyfulness early changed into worldly revelry, so the word came to be associated also with secular merry-making and traveling shows offering amusements. How and where is carnival still celebrated by churches.?

Cemeteries. Visit church and other cemeteries within reach. What are some of the oldest and most interesting graves and inscriptions? Tell something about several of the better-known persons buried there. Note unusual markers and changes in types through the years. Is one or more of the cemeteries of the no-monument kind? What do people in general think of these "burial parks"? Tell something of lot-selling, grave digging, funeral services, burial costs. Describe the work of cemetery caretakers.

Chaplains. Look into the history of armed service chaplaincies. How have chaplains borne up under fire as a rule? How do servicemen feel about them? Give examples. Describe the military chaplain's work in peacetime including chapel activities and counseling at home and overseas. Have churches grown up in unevangelized parts of the world as a result of outside work by chaplains? Is there opposition to the chaplaincy in some quarters because of possible infringement on the principle of separation of church and state? Interview chaplains, active and retired, if possible.

Other articles could deal with hospital and industrial chaplaincies.

Choirs. Describe striking points of interest and difference in choirs of representative local or area churches regarding size, directors, dress, amount of training, and expenses. Tell of churches with graded choirs for all ages. Are some of the choirs called upon for extra-church performances? Do they have concert tours, even abroad? How do pastors and members feel about the contribution of choirs to the total church program?

Christmas. Give examples to show that Christmas is not entirely commercialized. Do people feel that the uncertainty of actual date (birth of Jesus) and its connection with earlier non-Christian festivals make Christmas less Christian? What is the standing of Santa Claus today—with children, with adults? What about the exchange of gifts and Christmas greeting cards? Approximately what financial outlay is involved? How is the festival observed in different countries? How do Christians manage to celebrate it in communist and other lands where no holiday is allowed at work or in schools? Sketch historical development in the celebration of Christmas including, for instance, the influence of writings by Charles Dickens.

Communism. Approximately a third of the world's population is under communist rule. Is this taken account of in Christian mission strategy? Are missionaries legally in any communist lands? If not legally, how do they manage to stay there? Are others being trained for this work? What opportunities are offered by literature, radio? Compare and contrast Christianity and communism as to founder, sacred books, dogma, social concern, faith, eschatology. What can Christians learn from communists? Interview one or more of them if possible, or a converted former communist.

Comparative religion. Is knowledge of non-Christian religions more needed in the West today because of their mission work in Europe and America? Summarize and exemplify main teachings of principal world religions. Can Christianity fairly claim uniqueness? In what respects? A separate article could be prepared on each of the great world religions, with comparison to others and especially Christianity.

Converts. Give dramatic and non-dramatic examples of conversions from outside churches. What about those of young people and even small children? What methods used by churches are most effective in evangelism? Discuss the place of professional evangelists today and in the past. What do outsiders think of the church's evangelistic efforts; what do they find most attractive, most objectionable? Do churches receive applicants on request, after baptism or following a period of training in doctrine? Compare these methods with accounts of conversions in the book of Acts.

Contests. Ask Sunday school superintendents and others about prizes that have been offered, e.g. for learning books of the Bible, writing essays, enlisting largest number of new members, raising funds for building, winning in tournaments etc. Visit contests in sports, public speaking, music, drama, the locating of Bible passages and so on. What is the attitude of members towards such contests, and what results are indicated?

Crime. What percentage of convicted criminals came from actively religious homes, attended Sunday school and church? How frequent are convictions for crime by workers in the field of religion? Describe services in jails. Tell of some prisoners who have been converted, others who decided for the ministry while serving their sentences. What help is given by churches to ex-convicts?

Perhaps this is enough to impress you with the fact that feature ideas are everywhere and that there are pertinent questions to raise about any subject readers may be interested in. Each paragraph of suggestions above can be subdivided with additional questions in each part to make several articles.

Consider the following subjects also, any of which may be treated in relation to the field of religion. Still, these are only representative. The possibilities are endless.

Abortion, Accidents, Advent, Adventists, Adultery, Anabaptists, Ancestor Worship, Animals, Animism, Aging, Apocrypha, Asceticism, Auctions, Authority.

Bahaism, Bands, Baptism, Baptists, Basilicas, Bells, Benedictions, Bible Societies, Biblical Criticism, Biblical Societies, Bingo, Biography, Birth Control, Bishops, Blacks, Buddhism.

Calvinism, Canon Law, Catechisms, Charismatics, Charity Work, Christian Science, Church of Christ, Church of England, Church Government, Church and State, Church Growth, Church Year, Clerical Dress, Clothing, Clubs, Coffee Bars, Collections, Colleges, Communion, Concordance, Conferences, Confession, Confucianism, Conversion, Cooperation, Counseling, Creeds, Cross, Curators.

Dancing, Day of Atonement, Debates, Debts, Dedications, Democracy, Discipline, Disputes, Divorce, Doctors, Doctrine, Drama, Drinking, Drivers.

Easter, Eastern Orthodox Churches, Ecumenism, Elections, Electronics, Encyclopedias, Episcopalians, Eschatology, Ethical Culture Societies, Ethics, Evangelicals, Evangelists, Everyman.

Faith Missions, Family, Fasting, Father's Day, Fires, Floods, Flowers, Food, Friars, Fruit, Fundamentalism, Funerals.

Gambling, Gifts, Gnosticism, Godfathers.

Habits, Handbell Playing, Handicapped, Hanukkah,

Health, History Heresies, Hinduism, Hobbies, Holidays, Holiness Churches, Holy Week, Homosexuality, Hospitals, Hostels, House Churches, Houses of Worship, Humanism, Hymns, Hymnals.

Icons, Idolatry, Incarnation, Indians, Industry, Inquisition, Insurance, Islam, Israel.

Jainism, Jews, Journalism, Judges, Juvenile Delinquency.

Kindergartens, Kitchens, Koran, Ku Klux Klan.

Latter Day Saints (**Mormons**), Law, Laymen, Letters, Liberalism, Libraries, Literacy, Literature, Liturgy, Lord's Day, Lord's Supper.

Machines, Magazines, Magic, Mail, Manuscripts of Bible Books, Martyrs, Mass, Medical Missions, Medicine Men, Membership, Mental Hygiene, Methodists, Military Religious Orders, Ministers, Miracles, Mission, Modernism, Money, Moonism, Monuments, Morals, Moravian Church, Mosques, Mother's Day, Motion Pictures, Mottos, Museums, Music, Mythology.

Names, National Dress, Nature, Newspapers, New Year's Day, Nurses.

Oaths, Omens, Optimists, Orchestras, Outsiders.

Pacifism, Painting, Palestinians, Parking, Parochial Schools, Pastors, Patron Saints, Persecution, Photography, Pietism, Plymouth Brethren, Poetry, Police, Politicians, Pope, Population, Postal Services, Prophets, Presbyterians, Printing, Puritans.

Quakers, Quarrels, Quietism.

Rabbis, Radio, Rapture, Reading, Recipes, Records, Red Cross, Reformation, Reformed Churches, Relics, Religious Education, Religious Liberty, Retirement, Rewards, Roman Catholics, Rural Work.

Sabbath, Sacraments, Salaries, Salvation Army,

Sanatoriums, Science and Religion, Sculpture, Sewing Circles, Sects, Seekers, Seminaries, Sermons, Shinto, Shops, Slang, Slavery, Smoking, Socials, Stained Glass, Stamps, Stewardship, Suicides, Sunday, Sunday School, Symbolism.

Tabernacle, Talmud, Taxes, Temperance, Temple, Television, Thanksgiving Day, Theosophy, Tithing, Tourists, Tracts, Tradition, Travel, Transport, Trees, Transcendental Meditation.

Unitarianism, Universities, Uniforms, Unions, Unmarried Members, Ushers, United Churches, Upanishads, Utopias.

Valentine's Day, Vatican, Vehicles, Versions of the Bible, Vespers, Virgin Birth.

Waldenses, Wars of Religion, Weather, Weddings, Widows, Women's Ordination, Wood Carving, Worship.

Xylophones; YMCA, Yoga, Youth Work; Zealots, Zionism, Zoroastrianism.

Eight

Literature In A Hurry

Someone described journalism as "literature in a hurry." It produces its material on a daily or a weekly basis as a rule and has a brief, although influential, life. Writers have a limited period of time in which to prepare for frequent deadlines. Still, the pages of journalism have brought to the public eye much work that has endured.

Some literary figures who published part of their work in newspapers were: Joseph Addison, Richard Steele, Daniel Defoe, Benjamin Franklin, Mark Twain, O. Henry, Charles Dickens, Rudyard Kipling, William Faulkner and Ernest Hemmingway among others.

In writing for newspapers and magazines you should never feel that quality must be sacrificed. When you put a piece of writing in the mail or take it to your editor you should feel that it represents the best work you are capable of under the circumstances.

Opinion Articles. In editorials, by-lined pieces and regular columns there is often the opportunity to interpret events and express opinions that are not rightly allowable in news stories. It is best when the two functions are not confused. In many religion journals, unfortunately, almost every story reflects the bias of the sponsoring group.

You may have an opportunity to contribute to the editorial page or columns. Select those topics from the news that are timely and significant but which perhaps generate differences of opinion or cause confusion in the minds of readers. Do not avoid controversial matters. Be prepared to consider the issues thoroughly and give honest expression to your views. This assumes—particularly if you are writing for a partisan publication, denominational paper or "house organ"—that your approach to basic questions does not differ fundamentally from that represented by the publishing group.

You should have freedom to present the matter from your own point of view, but when the time comes that there is wide divergence between your beliefs and those of the publication in general, it is time for you to seek another market for your work.

Another section, often found on editorial pages, offers an open door of opportunity for the beginning writer. This is often headed simply "Letters to the Editor." Look through the news of the day, also editorials and bylined articles, and choose a topic on which you have a definite reaction. Write a letter to the editor expressing your feeling or opinion, or straighten him out on the facts. This is one of the easiest ways to break into print. Leading publications, especially the magazines, in some cases pay for letters that are used.

Reviews and criticism. Many newspapers and magazines publish book reviews as well as critical articles on drama, movies, music, painting, sculpture and architecture. There are occasional opportunities for religion writing in each of these fields.

How to prepare such material? Suppose you want to review a nonfiction book. The first thing is to look over the table of contents and the preface, then the introduction if there is one. Read the book as a whole, rapidly perhaps, for your own understanding and enjoyment. As you go along you may make light pencil markings by parts that particularly strike you, but don't try as yet to be critical. Give the author a chance.

After you have finished, reflect on what you have read. What was the main idea, or several leading ideas? Were these clearly analyzed and presented? Did the writing move smoothly from one part to the next and arrive at a tenable conclusion? If answers to these questions must be negative, or even if they are strongly positive, your criticism has begun.

Look now at the details. Reread some sections, maybe the entire book. Make full notes. What about the overall organization? Be sure to keep in mind, as the author certainly should, the readership for which it is intended.

In writing the book review your first job is to let your readers know what kind of work it is you are reviewing. Whether from quotations or summaries, probably both, the reader of the review must be given information on the contents of the book. He or she might appreciate some mention also about the author, his or her former work, how this book compares with earlier ones if any and with others on the subject. Give your judgment about what the author sought to accomplish, whether he did well and whether it was worth doing.

Avoid superlatives, either in commendation or derogation. Few books deserve them either way and their frequent use generally means lazy writing on the part of the reviewer. Take the trouble to be specific and selective.

You will usually need to be brief also. Many reviews are limited to a page or less of double-spaced typescript. List the name of the author, title and publication data (publisher, place of publication, date, pages and price) at the beginning. Many editors will not use all the publication data, but it is a simple matter for them to strike through parts they do not wish to publish.

Sometimes you may want to lump together several books which have recently come out in the same field and write a longer review article on the subject. This is more difficult for beginners. Try it after you have reviewed several individual books.

Curriculum material. An important aspect of the ministry of the church is the "teaching them" of Matthew 28:20. A congregation that takes seriously this part of the Great Commission will need not only Sunday schools and other church organizations but printed helps to give guidance and an abundance of material for various programs of work.

Many denominational and general publishing houses have a difficult time getting, in the form they need, the thousands of pages of manuscript material required each quarter for graded Sunday school classes, training groups, organizations for men, women, youth and children. One such publishing agency uses the work of about 1,900 free-lance part-time writers each year, bringing many of them to its central offices for instruction sessions and correlation of their work. This is a free trip, and writers are paid four or five cents a word for what they produce.

If you write for the Sunday schools, to take an example, you will need to be familiar not only with the biblical material but with the age group for which you prepare the material. If you have worked successfully with a certain age group, it is likely that you can write best for this age too.

Choose the publishing agency to which you would like to submit your manuscript and write a letter offering your services. Send along a sample of your work, perhaps the exposition of some passage for a particular age group in Sunday school just as you feel it might be publishable; or, if you have made this market somewhere before, send tear sheets of your work.

When you have a commission to undertake a block of curriculum writing, or just an invitation to submit material on speculation, be careful to follow instructions as to approach, illustrations, slant and length. And be sure to get the manuscript in on time. If you do a good job, other assignments will almost surely be forthcoming.

Inspirational writing. Many daily and weekly papers publish a brief feature of inspirational material in each issue, sometimes more. Religion journals have both short items and full-length articles of this nature. In addition, there are numerous quarterlies and books with devotional comments on a passage of scripture for each day.

Certainly this is a challenging field for religion writing. People by the millions are distraught with the complexities, the rush and the threats of our day. Many of them delight to find helpful thoughts in their reading that will enable them to look outward and upward, or which point the way toward more ethical behavior in daily life. They learn thankfully of religious truth and of the writer's spiritual experience which can illuminate a better way of life for them.

The great temptation for the writer of devotional materials is just to pass on what one has heard others say without giving time to fresh consideraton of the topic or Bible passage and attendant truth for daily living as it comes to him or her, and without taking pains to present it in a sincere and straightforward way. The beginning writer must guard against cheap sentimentality while giving at the same time proper place to genuine and restrained emotion. One must avoid the "language of Zion," which is pious words without real content, and embody thoughts in honest contemporary language.

Don't forget to use illustrations. Biblical truth is often obscured rather that revealed by abstruse logical analysis, whereas a simile or anecdote will illuminate it for the reader. Try for a neat balance. Your devotional writing should not be one story after another but ought to be based on sound exposition of the topic or passage. The illustration simply supplements this basic part of your task.

Remember to make the application also. This does not mean you always point the moral in so many words. It is best when you write the whole so as to make this unecessary. It is not a matter of indifference to you, however, whether the reader is affected in the least or not. You want real communication and response, mild as that response might be.

Sometimes sermons or devotional messages are published in magazines, or gathered together and published in book form. They are not generally suitable for publication as given orally, and need thorough revising and probably condensation, before submission to the editor. When a collection of messages is published in book form, it is better if they are on a single broad theme and comprise a logical whole.

Poetry. Poetry is characterized by intensity of feeling, serious reflection, economy and rhythm of expression. It brings images before our eyes, speaks both to heart and head. It deals with ideas, maybe old and ordinary ideas, but in a fresh and poignant way. The poem, especially the short lyric, is particularly suitable for the communication of spiritual truth.

Brief poems, including religious verse, are often welcomed by daily newspapers, sometimes just the Sunday edition, also by general and religion periodicals.

There is a place for doggerel and light verse, but do not confuse this with serious poetry. Whether you write in conventional forms with regular meter and rhyme, or in free verse that differs little from lined prose, let the poem express, in the most effective words you can find, your honest feelings about something that is significant, although it may have been suggested by a very small detail of life.

The writing of good hymns represents a real need in the realm of religion authorship. Until recently I would have said there is little place for free verse, but recent tunes have made extensive use of it. I would still say: Keep the meter regular as a rule and don't hesitate to use conventional rhyme if you feel like it. But, please, give some theological content. There seems to be less of a shortage of airy gospel songs just now than for genuine "odes of praise to Almighty God."

Fiction. The short story deals with a few characters involved in the solution of some problem or the working out of a situation. The novel is essentially the same, with more characters as a rule and perhaps several sub-plots. Almost always there is in the short story one main character, often with a single dominant trait, whom you make real to the reader by causing him or her to react consistently amid a developing situation that goes from bad to worse—then is resolved, usually through the efforts of your main character, in a reasonable and satisfying way.

Make the opposition force, whether people, nature or the main character's own desires, almost as strong as the one that will win out in the end. Show its power in succeeding scenes so that the opposition seems bound to win, although as the writer you must have in mind from the beginning how the problem is to be solved.

The short story may be as long as four or five thousand words, but those published in newspapers will more likely be "short shorts," perhaps around a thousand words. Religion journals prefer stories not more than 3,000 words as a rule, and the shorter ones sell much better, especially for the beginning writer.

The shorter the story the simpler it should be. This does not mean trivial themes for the short short. It does mean few characters, perhaps two or three. It means few scenes—which are marked by change in place or characters involved—maybe only one or two. It means little or nothing in the way of a sub-plot. In the short short there is not much room for character development, so you are almost obliged to take a "type," but try to make him or her individual enough to live.

As a writer in the field of religion you may be inclined to begin with "theme" as you look for a story idea. There is nothing wrong with this, except that you might wind up with more of a sermon than a story, and no editor wants this. Editors even of the Sunday school weeklies beg us not to send them "moralizing" stories. The moral will be there, but leave it implied. Show your reader in story action, instead of telling him or her outright, that love and faithfulness are great virtues. Pay most attention to strong character development, so far as there is room for it.

Plot is a bugaboo to most beginners, but if you have a believable situation calling for decision and action, you will get a plot willy nilly.

If you want to see a plot in the raw, read the comic strips. Even a four-frame sequence manages to get it in. This was illustrated in a wordless one I saw some time ago. The first scene was of a waiter carrying a tray of food, light lunch apparently, with a glass of iced tea and an apple for dessert. There is the situation.

The second frame showed the apple falling from the tray, which was being held with both hands. This was the complicating action, the problem. At this point the job of the author, whether cartoonist or writer, is to get the hero to solve his problem in a way which will be true to his character and satisfying to readers.

Frame three showed the waiter's effort to solve it. He caught the apple with his foot and kicked it back toward the tray.

But no solution in fiction must be too easy. There isn't room in the four-frame tableau, nor in the short short, for repeated trials and failures with final success. The cartoonist gave the story a half-tragedy ending, except that the issue isn't important so it makes comedy: the apple plumped down in the glass of tea.

You may be worried about how to get a plot in a thousand words or less. Now you have one from a cartoonist with no words at all. The difference is one of degree: In your story the main character, the **protagonist**, must face a significant problem of some sort and finally manage to solve it, despite tremendous opposition.

You had better write the story from the viewpoint of the main character. Don't ascribe to yourself omniscience and presume to say what is going on in the minds of all the characters. It will probably work out best if you limit yourself to relating what the main character could see or otherwise know about.

Take care with dialogue. Let the characters speak according to what they really are, not as professors of English even if in the story they haven't finished elementary school.

May you take real people as your models? You may, if you don't feel bound to reproduce them in toto, regardless of whether this fits your story or not. In creative writing you are the boss. Yours is the fault also if it doesn't jell. You can't ever blame the facts: "It really did happen that way!" This will not impress the editor at all.

Fiction should, I think, reveal the deepest facts of life; but particular characters, events, dialogue in the story—these must be yours. You can't put the responsibility on anyone else, or on history.

Usually your characters will be composites of various people you have known, even if you don't remember all of them individually as you write. Situations will be taken from other memories, and combinations. Even in writing fiction you have begun with people and events, somewhere down the line.

What comes out after several rewritings, however, will almost surely not be identifiable with particular acquaintances and happenings. But it should have the ring of truth in the little world you have created for your reader during the few minutes he spends with your story. You can even hope that his life will be influenced for good, even if it is a lighthearted story resulting only in the warmth of a smile.

Drama. The early history of drama was closely related to religion. Medieval miracle and morality plays sought to present biblical material in the beginning, but more and more the theatrical element predominated until drama occupied an entirely different world. It was then looked upon with disapproval by the church. Perhaps the principal demand for plays now, however, is in church and school.

The play, say an hour or two in length and divided into probably three acts, seeks to give more than a short story but less than a novel. The entire plot and character development must be revealed in dialogue and action on the stage. Conflict is even more intense as a rule than in the short story. There is the limitation of one-spot presentation, and a short play should have only one or two settings. These should be simple too, if the piece is to be produced in churches.

Still, there are advantages in play writing. You don't have to worry about descriptions and exposition, except as this occurs in dialogue. It won't be extensive there, for units of dialogue should be true to life and therefore brief. Don't take the liberties of Shakespeare and put long speeches in the mouths of your characters.

If you are good at noting the way people speak and can get several of them into trouble and out again, with strong feeling revealed in the conflict, play writing may be your forte. Try it. It can be a farce, tragedy or melodrama; local, biographical or from church history. Mission work offers interesting material for church drama.

Denominational and interdenominational publishing houses want plays, and there are publishers who major in this form, secular and religious. See writers' yearbooks and market guides for addresses, listing of requirements and payment.

Try to have your play produced a few times before submitting it for publication. You will be able to improve it in the process, as you note parts of the dialogue and action which are well received by the audience and other parts that do not seem to go over. If there isn't a drama group in your church, maybe you can organize one.

Writing scenarios for films is a limited field in the world of religion; but there are several companies, denominational and nondenominational, that produce such dramatic works.

Radio and Televison. Many writers consider radio a lost cause since the advent of television. Not so. There are more radio broadcasting stations than ever before, and radio is just coming into its own in some parts of the world. You may or may not be paid for religion materials to be used on radio or television, but there are many opportunities to reach people for good.

The typical religion radio program is perhaps a brief sermon or devotional talk. It will probably be much more effective if written out carefully with the medium in mind, and some stations require this. Be modest in the number of ideas you try to get across in the few minutes available. Make words and sentences short, not too pious. Repeat the main idea, each time in a slightly different way. Use brief but striking illustrations.

Remember that many of your listeners are driving along the highway—or having breakfast, reading the morning paper and saying good morning to the wife all at the same time, while the speaker's voice is coming over the air. This may seem pretty hopeless, but still it is possible perhaps to get something across to your busy listener.

Religious music will be used in connection with the radio programs. There are of course many which are largely or exclusively music, but even where the script is minimal it should be well prepared.

If you are interested in news broadcasting, see if you can

get a fifteen-minute spot once a week on your local station to review religion developments of the past several days, perhaps with some interpretation and analysis.

There are many further possibilities such as interviewing interesting personalities in religion on a regular or occasional radio or television program. Book reviewing is another activity adapted to these media. It can be combined in some cases with the interview, if there are authors within reach whose books you would like to review on the air.

Dramatic presentations, formerly popular on radio, have unfortunately been taken over almost entirely by television, insofar as the United States is concerned. I say unfortunately because radio is still a potent medium for drama, as evidenced by Radio Mystery Theater and a few other continuing programs. If skillfully done, it can in many cases be more powerful even than plays on television. The listener, if he or she will devote attention to it without distractions, can become more involved than with a television presentation because one is called upon to use the imagination more.

Take full advantage also of increased opportunities in writing for television. Movements will be acted out in this medium instead of described or suggested. Dialogue is a bit different. Facial expressions are important. Bright pageantry or musty old buildings may contribute to mood. Dress and staging are important, whereas they play no part on radio.

TV drama must be hard-hitting, concentrated, with a simple though significant theme and plot. Pregnant possiblities for material include dramatic occurrences in church history, the lives of outstanding Christians, other religions, contemporary events in church life, the usual worship services, large gatherings and dramatic ecclesiastical rites.

Miscellaneous. There are probably opportunities for your writing even in the bulletin of your local church. If there is not a church paper of some sort, perhaps you can get one started. It should carry announcements, news of church activities and perhaps a short column by the pastor or other member of the staff. Brief feature articles could report visits to one department then another of the Sunday school and other organizations of the church, its mission station, recreational programs, sports and so on. There might be news and occasional articles about other churches and groups in the community, state, nation and world—very selective, of course, but a few interesting items now and then.

The writing of evangelistic and other tracts challenges the free lance. This is sometimes remunerated, sometimes not, but here again the real pay-off is in the many lives that may be changed for the better by testimony you can give as a religion writer.

Almost every newspaper and periodical uses "fillers." These may be epigrams, striking quotations, verse couplets or quatrains, brief pieces of interesting information up to about one manuscript page are printed. Editors welcome such material to fill the remaining space on a page at the conclusion of a feature article or story, and some readers turn to these short pieces first of all. The filler is an ideal form for the beginner in writing and the part-time free lance who can find only snatches of time in which to work.

Brief articles used by church bulletin services may be short,but they are the features of the bulletin. Usually the bulletin service prepares only the outside pages of a single folded sheet, with an appropriate illustration for the season on the first page and these printed "features" (one or two, as a rule) on the back page. On the two inside pages the local church prints or mimeographs the program of its worship services for the day, announcements etc. A copy of the bulletin is given to each person attending the services.

"A man would have to preach to 450 people every Sunday for 50 years to speak to as many persons as the author of one bulletin article," stated the editor of a denominational bulletin service some time ago. That meant more than a million potential readers of the material. Such an opportunity is worthy of one's best effort, aside from the fact that it is paid for—about six cents a word, in this case.

It is quite true, as I have said, that in fiction you are totally responsible for creative writing and cannot be saved by the appeal, "It really happened." It is also true, however, that some incidents in biography and history are so dramatic that you will only need to create a bit of dialogue and perhaps telescope events somewhat to make good "fact fiction." Here is such a story, which I sold to the youth paper *Upward;* it was published November 1, 1959. It sold also to another paper in the form of a one-act drama. (Adoniram Judson became America's pioneer foreign missionary, serving in Burma.)

"Also In Me"

At dusk on a September day in 1808 Adoniram Judson rode up to the inn in a Connecticut village and turned his horse over to an attendant.

He strode into the hallway of the frame building. Despite slight build, his manner was one of self confidence, his stride long and firm. Finding no one at the reception desk he began to shout.

"Hello!" he called. "Hello! Who's running this place?"

"I'm coming," the answer drifted down, clearly but in a subdued tone, from upstairs.

Adoniram heard the labored movements of someone coming hurridly down the stairs, and within half a minute the corpulent form of a middle-aged man appeared.

Greetings were exchanged, and Judson asked for a room.

"I'm sorry, sir," said the innkeeper apologetically, but I have only one room left. I'm afraid it would not suit you."

"Why not?"

"Oh, the room's all right," explained the innkeeper, "but it's next door to one occupied by a young man who is ill. He arrived several hours ago and became seriously ill almost immediately."

"I understand," said Adoniram. "I shall take care to make no unnecessary noise."

"Oh, I'm not thinking of that," the innkeeper corrected. "It's you I'm thinking of. The doctor and others will be attending him. I'm afraid you would be disturbed by sounds from the sick chamber."

"Don't let that bother you," smiled Adoniram. "I am a very sound sleeper, and now I'm tired enough to sleep in the middle of a hurricane if necessary. Will you show me to the room?"

"Gladly, sir," said the innkeeper. "First will you please sign your name here in my register?" He dipped a pen in the inkwell and handed it to Adoniram.

"J'sn's the name," Adoniram mumbled. "You write it down for me. I'll be getting my things together here."

The innkeeper was obviously surprised at this request, and he watched Adoniram elaborate as much as possible the simple task of picking up a small pair of saddlebags. Then he quickly turned his attention to the registry book.

"Mr. Johnson, is it?" He began a slow deliberate writing out of the name.

"No need to put a first one," Adoniram commented. "Just write "A.' "

"Mr. . . . A . . . John . . . son," said the innkeeper to himself as he wrote out the words with care. "Mr. A. Johnson," he repeated as he surveyed his handiwork. "And the address?"

"Now that's a good question," Adoniram laughed, putting the saddlebags on the floor again and seating himself in a chair nearby. "A good question," he mused, half to himself. "Perhaps I shall be able to tell you after I have completed my present journey." He laughed again, but obviously without much amusement. "For the present you may just put Plymouth."

"May I ask, Mr. Johnson, what your business is? It is not necessary for you to say, but usually I note this too in my book. Perhaps I could venture a guess. It is a pleasant diversion of mine to guess the profession of my guests.

"Venture it then by all means," said Adoniram with a scarcely noticeable touch of impatience. "Then you will please show me to my room."

"Yes, sir, of course," the friendly innkeeper assured his guest. "This will take no more than a minute. I think you must be a poet, maybe still in college or another profession, but really a poet?"

"Ha! you missed it this time," laughed Adoniram. After a pause he spoke in a more serious tone. "Here you have raised another good question, Mr. Landlord, to which there is no proper answer. What am I? I would really like to know."

"But you are surely a literary person of some kind, aren't you sir, or an artist?"

"Well, maybe," replied Adoniram thoughtfully. "I graduated from Brown University just over a year ago, and during the past session I taught school in my home town. As for being a writer, I have done a couple of books, but they were on grammar and mathematics—far from poetry as you guessed. My most recent occupation has been playwrighting, in New York. So what *is* my occupation? I suppose, after all, your guess is as good as mine."

"Very interesting, sir," said the innkeeper, as he took Adoniram's saddlebags in one hand and a burning candle in the other and led the way up the stairway.

Near the end of the hall on the second floor the innkeeper put down the saddlebags and opened a door.

"Will you be wanting a call in the morning, sir?" asked the innkeeper as he entered the room with the saddlebags and placed the candle on a bedside table.

"Yes, and hot water for shaving," Adoniram responded. "At six-thirty. You'll fodder my horse and tuck him in for the night? I shall continue my journey westward tomorrow."

"Of course, Mr. Johnson. Is there anything else?"

"No, nothing else." Adoniram threw off his coat, loosened his shirt and sank with a sigh into an old easy chair in one corner of the room.

The innkeeper lingered in the doorway. "There's a Bible on the table," he said, "in case you would like to read before retiring. I've watched folks here a long time and those who read it seem to sleep better than the others."

"Bible? Ha! No, I certainly won't need *that*. 'Happy is he who reclineth not on revelation's fancy,' Jacob used to say."

"Jacob said that? I do not recall such a passage."

"I'm sorry," Adoniram apologized. "I was just talking to myself, not referring at all to the Jacob of whom you are thinking. Just a friend of mine at Brown. Clever fellow, Jake. President of our deist club."

"Deist? That's that French atheism, isn't it?"

"Atheism, no!" Adoniram protested. "We believe in God. He is the great First Cause. Reason tells us that. But we don't try to drag God into man's affairs. That would be dishonoring to the great Creator. Also, I can assure you, deism is quite American now."

"That may be," said the older man, sadly. "I don't understand all those things. But I hold to my Bible. You deists don't make much of the Bible, do you?"

Adoniram shrugged indifferently "The Bible's all right, where it corresponds to reason and natural morality. It's that belief of people in special revelation, miracles and salvation through the death of someone nearly eighteen centuries ago that does damage to the human spirit."

"I'm sorry to hear you say that, sir," said the innkeeper, in obvious distress. "I can't answer your philosophies, but . . . I'm sorry . . . ."

"Oh, that's all right. Don't let it bother you." Adoniram realized he was troubling the good man unnecessarily. "As a matter a fact, my father is a clergyman. He believes as you do. He and my mother were terribly hurt when they found out about my views a few weeks ago. But after all, a man must be true to himself."

"That's right, Mr. Johnson. A man must be true to himself, his very deepest self. He must be true to that, or he'll never find any peace. Excuse me, sir." The innkeeper turned to leave. "Supper will be in a quarter of an hour," he said.

For a moment Adoniram was taken aback by what the man had said, but he quickly recovered his confident manner. "Yes, of course," he echoed the innkeeper's words. "That's it. True to one's real self. That's what Jake and I always said."

Just then, for the first time, Adoniram heard groans from the adjoining room and sounds of one or more persons walking about.

"Pretty bad off, is he?" asked Adoniram of the innkeeper, who still stood in the doorway. He motioned toward the sickroom.

"Indeed he is. Doctor says he will probably not last out the night."

"That *is* bad," said Adoniram.

"I really hope that it will not disturb you too much, Mr. Johnson," said the innkeeper with honest concern.

"Is there anything I can do to help?" asked Adoniram.

"Nothing at all, thank you," the innkeeper answered. "The doctor is there most of the time, and there are watchers to take turns during the night."

"Then I shall not give it another thought," boasted the younger man. "To do so under such circumstances would be sheer sentimentality. We do not want that, do we?"

"No," said the innkeeper unhappily. "I suppose not." He left.

Adoniram bathed his face and hands from the water bowl in his room, tidied up a bit and went down to supper. He sat at a small table by himself and had practically no conversation with the innkeeper or anyone else.

Back in his room, tired and grateful for privacy at last, he piddled for a long time among the things in his saddlebags then removed his outer clothing and threw himself across the bed to rest.

Groans started coming again from the sickroom, and Adoniram discovered to his chagrin that he was not nearly as untroubled as he had claimed in speaking with the innkeeper. As minutes stretched into hours, his thoughts clamored for attention and banished sleep.

The landlord had said the poor sufferer would probably not last out the night. Was he prepared to die? Adoniram felt a blush of shame creep over him at the question, for it seemed to prove the shallowness of his philosophy. What would his friends at Brown University say to his weakness? What would the clear-minded, intellectual, witty Jacob Eames say to such boyishness?

The sounds continued to come from the other room, and Adoniram's thoughts kept reverting to the sick man—despite his efforts to forget the whole business and go to sleep. Was the sufferer a Christian, calm and strong in the hope of a glorious immortality, or shuddering on the brink of eternity unprepared?

Perhaps he was a freethinker, educated by Christian parents and prayed over by a Christian mother. The innkeeper had described him as a young man, and in his imagination Adoniram was forced to place himself upon the deathbed, although he strove with all his might to prevent it.

Adoniram did not know later whether he had slept more than a few minutes at rare intervals throughout the night. But morning came at last, and the bright flood of light which poured into his room dispelled all his "superstitious illusions" of the night.

He heard no sounds from the sickroom. Perhaps the young man's condition was not as bad as had been thought. Maybe a painful case of indigestion or something of the sort had caused his severe discomfort during the night.

Adoniram went to the mirror and laughed at his sorry appearance. Whistling to boost his spirits, he washed his face vigorously, shaved, jerked on clothing, combed his hair and started for the door. Then there was a knock on it.

"Come in," he called out.

"Good morning, Mr. Johnson," the innkeeper greeted him. "It is six-thirty, and your breakfast will be ready in a few minutes." He put a pitcher of fresh water on the stand.

"Good morning!" said Adoniram brightly. "Thank you." There was a pause. Then Adoniram said. "My neighbor seems to be better this morning. Very quiet now."

"He is dead, sir," said the innkeeper solemnly.

"Dead!" gasped Adoniram, revealing his concern. "I'm sorry. Do you know who he was?"

"Yes," replied the other man, "a Mr. Eames, Mr. J. C. Eames."

"Jake Eames *here? dead?*" exclaimed Adoniram, as he dashed out and threw open the door to the next room, darting to the bedside. With a mumbled apology to the astounded man seated nearby, Adoniram jerked back the sheet that covered the body on the bed.

"Yes, it's Jake!" he exclaimed, then stumbled back into his own room.

The innkeeper had followed Adoniram as far as the doorway of Eames's room, and he now returned with his troubled guest.

"I'm sorry, sir," he said. "Can I do anything?"

"Yes," Adoniram managed to answer. "Please try to get word to his father in Bellford. You'll take care of things here, I'm sure, until he arrives.

"I'll see to it, sir."

"And there is one other thing you can do for me." He pointed to the Bible, which remained unopened on the table.

"Read me something, please."

"Yes, sir," said the surprised innkeeper. "Right gladly will I do that for you." He opened the volume and leaved thoughtfully through it.

"Yes," he mused, smoothing the leaves down at a well-worn page, "nothing like John 14 for times like these."

He began to read, "Let not your heart be troubled: ye believe in God, believe also in me . . . ."

"Stop there," Adoniram broke in. He was standing by the window staring thoughtfully out on the village street. "That's the next step. That's the next step for me. Believe in God . . . . Even the deist says that. But he doesn't understand it. And it is not enough. It's not enough, Jake, for times like this. It's not enough to live by and not enough to . . . die by. We put God too far away, Jake, and so he's not here to help us.

" 'Also in me.' Perhaps in him we can see God as he really is, Jake. In him who said, 'Believe also in me.'"

Adoniram began packing his saddlebags.

"You are leaving at once, sir? asked the innkeeper.

''Yes, Adoniram replied. "There's nothing I could do here.

Tell Mr. Eames I'll come for the funeral. In the meantime there is unfinished business for me in Plymouth. I must confess to my dear parents what a fool I have been."

Then he stopped and looked questioningly at the innkeeper. "Do you think they will receive me, after the way I've acted?"

"I'm sure they will, Mr. Johnson," was the confident and smiling reply. "I'm sure they will."

"And there's another thing," said Adoniram. "I can begin my confession here with you. My name is not Johnson, but Judson. When I left home I was determined to see 'life,' as I expressed it, 'the dark side as well as the bright.' I joined a desreputable theatrical company which was touring New York state. I was no better than the rest of them, drinking, carousing, leaving towns we played in without paying board bills and all that sort of thing.

"I didn't want to bring reproach on my family, and I wished complete freedom for myself; so I never spoke my name distinctly, never wrote it down. Everyone took it for 'Johnson,' and I let it go at that."

Adoniram looked earnestly and appreciatively into the eyes of the innkeeper and firmly clasped his hand. "Thank you," he said, "thank you very much. Now I'll go in for a last look at Jake."

Adoniram walked slowly to the adjoining room, stood for a moment in the doorway, shuffled over to the bed on which the body lay and raised the sheet slightly to reveal the pale face of his departed friend.

"Also in me," Adoniram mused in solemn tones. Unaccustomed tears filled his eyes and his voice broke. "Also in me.' We missed that part, Jake, that all-important part. Ours wasn't enough, Jake. I'll testify to that to the ends of the earth if I can: 'Believe in God, believe also in me.' "

Nine

What's Your Style?

Perhaps you are frightened away from useful work you should be doing for publication because you are "just not a writer." By this you may mean you cannot write in the colorful style you associate with authorship. Actually there is no particular way of writing, even that of the finest author you know, which you should imitate. Writing is as individual as a fingerprint. Write, at least in the first draft, as you would in penning a letter or speaking with a friend. Then revise and rewrite as needed.

There are of course a few basic principles one needs to keep in mind. The first is to state your idea clearly. Some knowledge of grammar will help in this. But if you can speak and write clearly without being able to formulate a single one of the rules, this is nearly as good. It would mean that you have developed a built-in sense of grammar even though you may be unconscious of it.

If phrases and clauses tend to go off in all directions for you, however, and verbs refuse to match their subjects, it might be good for you to get a simple grammar book and give yourself a few lessons.

Rather than spending your energy in dressing up your writing to achieve some imagined "style," simplify it. This doesn't mean you regard anything beyond a two-syllable word as unclean. Just that you prefer the simple word to the complicated one. That heavy artillery from the unabridged dictionary should carry a lot of meaning, beyond what simpler expressions would, to justify its use. Even then you should mentally check your reader's vocabulary and be sure what you have written wouldn't be gobbledygook to him. This will vary greatly according to what you are writing about and for what group of readers.

Favoring the simpler expression need not mean weak and colorless writing. The common words, rooted as they are in the life of a people, are usually the most forceful. The concrete and specific words are better than the abstract and general ones as a rule.

Make your verbs carry the ball when you can, rather than adjectives and adverbs. Eliminate some of those manifold appearances of "to be," "seem" and other such feeble connectives. If you have a fairly equal choice between active and passive voice, take the active. Strive for fresh and original figures of speech rather than parroting all the old cliches.

Benjamin Franklin, that early American master of effective prose, said that writing should be smooth as well as short and simple. You will probably discover that you tend to a certain rhythm in your own writing style, without giving particular thought to it. If not, you might experiment with some of your sentences that seem particularly jerky or unbalanced, and try to improve them.

You will need to guard against length and unnecessary complications in sentences and paragraphs as well as words. If you find a sentence meandering beyond 40 or 50 words, stop and ask yourself, "Is this trip necessary?" You will probably discover that several short excursions would make everybody happier—you, the editor and your readers. Fairly long sentences may justify themselves occasionally by avoiding numerous repetitions of subject, object or their pronouns.

Remember: paragraphs also—not too long. In journalistic writing you start a new one at the least provocation. And provocations come quickly to the average reader faced with a block of print in a narrow column stretching way down the page of his newspaper.

Ideas are grasped more quickly when they are not all jammed together. Many newswriters like paragraphs under a hundred words as a rule, and half that is sometimes enough for these monitors of "literature in a hurry." Editors of magazines and books generally give you more leeway, and in writing for them you can let the paragraph develop an idea as it is commonly supposed to do.

Within the limits chosen, vary the length both of sentences and paragraphs. This makes for rhythm in writing as a whole.

In addition to the use of the word "style" to refer to one's individual way of writing, it is used also in a more limited sense. Here it has to do with the mechanics of writing and printing and includes such things as spelling, abbreviations, capitalization and punctuation.

There is wide variety of usage in these matters. The ideal solution is perhaps to find out the way each editor wants it and prepare material to be sent to him according to his rules. This is next to impossible, however, if you submit to many different markets. The best practicable plan is to follow the style sheet of the market you write most for, adapting it perhaps at a few points according to your own convictions.

You may take it as your basic principle, for instance, that you will use minimum capitalization and punctuation so long as clarity and good taste are not sacrificed. To give yourself some defense when people knock you over the head with an old rule book, you might make it another condition that you have at least one good authority.

Say you are following in general the Associated Press Stylebook (it is avilable at nominal cost, or in a good library), but you want to write "communist" without a capital letter. When the purists descend on you, pull out a copy of *Reader's Digest* and state without equivocation that this most successful journal, with the widest circulation of any, consistently follows the same practice. So do many others.

Likewise you may decide to make "pope" lower case, as do many publishers, "biblical" and "scriptural" also. Your real reason is not that you want to downgrade the pope or the Bible, although some readers seem to take it this way. You just don't like the tendency to weaken the capital by overusing it. As with any other product, oversupply reduces value. And having many capitals slows down typing, even reading.

Some people feel they do honor to God by capitalizing all pronouns and many adjectives referring to him. This practice can lead to considerable confusion in reading, especially when the subject is biblical or theological and so many of the words seem to qualify for capitalization. I seriously doubt that the writer receives extra credit for it in the heavenly ledgers.

Be moderate in your use of punctuation also. Too much of it makes for jerky writing and reading that is out of harmony with journalistic style especially. As always, the basic rule is clarity.

Suggestions for a Style Sheet

Captials. Except for unimportant conjunctions, articles

and prepositions, start each word with a capital in the following cases:

1. Titles preceding a name (and the proper name itself of course), if they are really used as titles, not those following a name and not "invented" titles.

Examples: President Smith, doctor of divinity; Donald Ayland, president since 1978; senior member Peter Johnson.

2. Institutions, organizations, political parties, courts, armies, wars, periods of history, commissions and important standing committees perhaps—if full and proper name of the thing is used, or if part is used specifically to represent the whole and might not be so understood unless it is capitalized.

Examples: Bethany Christian College, which is the college that . . . ; Religious News Service . . . the Service . . . World War II. There are some permissible exceptions such as: the second world war.

3. Decorations and awards: Nobel Peace Prize . . . the prize.

4. Holidays: New Year's Day . . . to begin the new year . . .

5. Periods of history: Middle Ages (middle ages o.k. too), Gay Nineties.

6. Titles of books, articles, hymns, poems, stories.

Capitalize as a rule initial letters of all words except articles and short prepositions (these also if they come first or last).

7. Scripture (lower case also permissible), the Word (Christ or Bible), but it is not necessary to capitalize: heaven, hell, devil, biblical.

8. Regions of the earth (the nouns are almost always

capitalized and usually the adjectives also): the West, Eastern cultures, Siberia.

9. Initial letter in first word of full quoted sentence after introductory phrase: John Robinson said, "The Lord has yet more truth to break forth out of his holy Word."

10. Occasionally a capital letter may be used for unusual effect, sometimes with the suggestion of irony or pomposity: Almost everyone wants to be a Writer but few will discipline themselves and write regularly.

Abbreviations: Mr., Prof., Ms., Dr., B.D., D.D., Th.M., Ph.D.; Gen. (General, Genesis), Matt., U.S.S.R., U.S., Oct. 23, B.C., A.D., Mt. Everest, A.M., P.M. (or a.m., p.m.). Most of these abbreviations, especially those consisting entirely of capitals, may also be used without the periods. Always spell out titles and books of the Bible when used separately, e.g., Speak to the professor about the assignment in Genesis.

Punctuation. The period is used at the end of a declarative sentence, with abbreviations (exceptions indicated above) and to separate parts of a decimal number such as 205.32.

The comma comes between long independent clauses joined by a simple conjunction(and, but, for, neither, nor), separates words in apposition and parenthetical expressions, follows some adverbial modifiers and other phrases as well as dependent clauses introducing a sentence, divides long figures into threes and words or phrases in series. In journalistic style commas are normally not used after names preceding Jr. (or jr.) and Sr. or place identifications.

Examples: John Mapelton Jr. of New York and the Rev. T.I. Jones, pastor in Durham . . . 2,947,562. If he gets to go, she refuses to.

The semicolon is sometimes useful to separate phrases and especially clauses which come together without a conjunctive word or have an adverbial conjunction. Occasionally the semicolon is used even when clauses are joined by a simple conjunction if these clauses are very long or have internal punctuation. Avoid such constructions where possible in journalistic writing, or just use a comma instead of a semicolon if the sense is clear. Rules were made for writing, not writing for rules.

The colon follows formal introduction to listed material. It is also used in clock time and Bible quotations.

Examples: Several organizations cooperate in the project: (the dash could be used instead of the colon here) the women's society, men's organization, Sunday school and the youth group. 7:42 p.m., Gal. 2:20.

In forming the possesive the apostrophe comes before the "s" of most singular and a few plural nouns, after it in ordinary plurals. When the singular already ends in "s" an apostrophe with another "s" may be used if the word (usually a name) is a short one. To a polysyllabic singular ending in "s," just add the apostrophe. With individual letters and numbers the apostrophe is sometimes used before the "s" to form the plural, but the trend is to omit it wherever possible. It, is incorrect to use the apostrophe in forming the plural of family names.

Examples: Tom's house. Charles's undertaking. Klinkerscales' name. Men's group. Preachers' families. The 2's or 2s, W's or Ws but the m's and s's. The Smiths, not Smith's. Exceptions: In Jesus' name, Moses' law. For conscience' sake.

Quotation Marks. Put them at the beginning and end of quoted material, as well as around the titles of books, articles, plays and so on. (In formal writing for periodicals and books italics are used for titles of books, names of newspapers and magazines; these are indicated in manuscript by underlining.)

Quotation marks also sometimes denote slang, words used in an irregular way or in reference to themselves; but such usage should be minimized.

Use single marks for quote within a quote. Always put the comma and the period inside quotation marks, if you want to follow U.S. usage. Other punctuation should be placed logically according to construction of the sentence.

Example: "Hear and heed the command, 'Go ye,'" said the speaker. The article "Religion in Russia" was reprinted as part of a book by the same title.

The hypen is used to divide a word at the end of a line and to join words used as one. Be sure not to divide a syllable, and don't leave a one-letter syllable standing all alone. Write combination words "solid" wherever possible and avoid too many divisions at the end of lines—the righthand margin does not have to be straight.

Examples: The man-eating shark was killed (without the hyphen the meaning is different). Secretary-treasurer. Ex-president. Dateline. Cooperate.

The Dash. This "double-hyphen" (on the typewriter) indicates a break in the statement: He did his best—and no one's best was better—to play a good game.

The exclamation point. It follows a strong ejaculation. Use it sparingly. Example: Look out for that car!

Parentheses. These marks inclose explanatory material or that which is not properly a part of the text. (Square brackets and footnotes are seldom used in journalism.) Punctuate according to whether the parenthetical matter is part of the main sentence.

Example: Johnson was the third man to serve in that capacity (the others were James P. Samuels and Conrad Meyer).

Ten

Manuscript To Market

Make yourself a market list of papers and magazines you would like to write for and keep it up to date. List the name of each publication, editor, address, frequency of issue, types of material and length desired, whether photocopied manuscripts are acceptable, whether these may be submitted to other markets at the same time with indication on each that this is being done, amount of payment, and whether it is "on acceptance" or "after publication."

Where are you to get this information? Some of it you can obtain from study of the publications themselves. Many periodicals have instruction sheets or pamphlets for prospective writers. Send for these and ask for sample copies of the publications you do not otherwise have access to. The helps for writers are almost always furnished free, often the sample copies also. You may want to write to editors with specific questions about their needs.

Your principal source for the needed information may be market lists in writers' magazines such as *The Writer* (8 Arlington Street, Boston, Massachusetts 02116) and *Writer's Digest* (9933 Alliance Road, Cincinnati, Ohio 45242). The listing in each issue will cover markets of a certain type, e.g., general magazines, trade, journals, short story markets, newspaper syndicates, outdoor life, sports, poetry, juveniles or publications in the field of religion.

Book publishers are listed also. Over the period of a year or so there will be a rather complete listing of markets in these writers' magazines.

There are annual or occasional volumes also, covering all kinds of markets, e.g. *Writer's Market* published by *Writer's Digest* and *The Writer's Handbook* by *The Writer*. *The Successful Writers and Editors Guidebook* was published by Creation House in 1977 and it is intended for writers in the field of religion. In Britain, *The Writers' and Artists' Yearbook* is published regularly by Adam and Charles Black, London. Don't neglect the British market!

Some writers make a practice of querying editors in advance as to whether they are interested in certain article ideas. There is almost never any point in your sending a query about fiction, and if you are a real beginner perhaps not much need for it in regard to articles.

Writers who have an established reputation, even of a modest or local sort, can save time by writing to editors after they have assembled some material but before the article has been put into final form. The editor, if he is interested, can suggest specifically what he wants and how treated. Then when the manuscript reaches his desk he will consider it more carefully and sympathetically perhaps than that stack of unsolicited stuff on his desk which came in "cold" or "over the transom" without any previous contact. When you get the "go-ahead" from an editor or assistant editor, address any further correspondence and also the finished manuscript to him or her personally.

After completion of the first or second draft of your article or fiction story it might be good to put it aside for a few days and work on something else. You can come back to it then with some freshness and objectivity. Keep several projects in the mill at the same time so that you do not remain idle while one is laid aside.

One of the most important elements in your development as a writer is learning to be your own critic. Letting someone else read your material is helpful too, if he or she will be honest with you and if you are willing to profit by the criticism.

In the last analysis, of course, you must make the decisions. Imagine yourself the reader, then the editor. Go through your article or story as if you were the other person. Regard nothing you have set down on paper as sacred or final. Be ruthless with yourself in cutting out material if it does not contribute to your specific purpose, or if the piece is longer than the editor wants.

In typing out the final copy, write your name and address in the upper left-hand corner of page 1, leaving normal margins. Just across on the right side of the same page write "Fiction" or "Article" and the approximate number of words. Skip down then maybe a third of the page (to give the editor room for his instructions to the printer) and write the title in capitals, under that the byline with your name or pen name. Then begin the article or story, leaving margins of about an inch and a quarter on the left side of each page, a little less than that on the right side, top and bottom.

At the upper right on each page after the first put your last name or some main words of the title, perhaps both, along with the page number. This will help the editor get your manuscript back together again if the sheets become separated among the stacks of manuscripts and other papers piled on his desk.

At the end of the article or story put "End." The conclusion of a news story is usually indicated by "30" (don't ask me why!) or some other arbitrary symbol such as

#, with "more" at the bottom of preceding pages (note, this is only for news copy).

Be sure to keep a carbon or photocopy of everything, marking on it, or in a notebook you keep for the purpose, the name of each publication to which you send the manuscript, date etc. Later you will write down another date beside the original entry indicating whether the piece was accepted or rejected and if accepted the payment made.

If your manuscript adds up to not more than five or six pages, you can fold it twice and mail it in a long narrow envelope. From approximately seven to fifteen pages, fold it once and use a larger envelope. If there are more pages than that, mail flat, preferably with a cardboard sheet on one side to keep it that way.

You should generally inclose a second envelope, addressed to yourself, with sufficient postage for return of the manuscript in case it is not accepted for publication; this is the "SASE" (Self Addressed Stamped Envelope) you see indicated for almost all publications in the market lists. Otherwise the editor is under no obligation to acknowledge or return what you sent him. Don't count on his doing it out of goodwill. Even if he does, he will have less goodwill in the consideration of your next submission.

With manuscripts sent abroad you may inclose international postal coupons, purchased at the post office, or your personal check for the small amount that seems to be indicated.

The payment of return postage applies to material sent on speculation. If you have a definite assignment, or if your piece has no value except for the particular market, you need not send postage.

What about agents? Writers speak endlessly on the pros and cons of using them. Many professionals market all their work through agents, who submit the material to editors and bargain for the best rates possible. The agent keeps 10 percent (more for overseas sales, movies etc.), and doubtless this is a good investment for writers who can use the time that is saved to produce more for high-paying markets. However, it is very difficult to get a good agent to represent the novice or part-time author.

For almost all part-time religion writers the question of agents need not arise. If you are good enough to have one, they will probably be looking for you. Rates paid in the religion field, although rising, are generally not high enough to attract reputable agents. In case you would like to get in touch with an agent, however, consult the listing that gives their addresses and interests in one of the market manuals named above. Maybe one will represent you.

You can probably market your work nearly as well as an agent could, provided you give sufficient time to it. Just spend some time studying the market lists and reading the journals and papers you wish to write for, then send your manuscripts to the editors who would likely be most interested in what your are producing. If your efforts are returned to you, get them out to other possible markets, rewriting in the meantime as may be needful.

Should you write a letter to accompany the manuscript? Yes, if you have something to say. There doesn't seem to be much point in writing the editor that you are sending him such and such manuscript and hope he will consider it for publication. That much is obvious when he gets the article or story from you.

If you are unknown to the editor and have special

qualifications for just the sort of material you have prepared, write the editor informing him of your qualifications and your experience in the field, mentioning any previous writings you may have had published.

Make up your mind from the beginning that you will not be unduly discouraged by printed rejection slips you may begin to accumulate. Editors do not have time to write individual letters to all those whose material is not accepted. If you do get such a letter, be careful to profit to the utmost from any suggestions given, whether you are to submit the piece to the same market again or to another.

And remember—keep your writings in the mail!

Selected Bibliography

Brodie, W. Austin, *Keeping Your Church in the News*. Westwood, N.J.: Fleming H. Revell Company, 1959, pp. 125.

Osteyee, Edith Tiller, *Writing for Christian Publications*. Philidelphia: The Judson Press, 1953, pp. 206.

Porter, Roy E. and others, *The Writer's Manual*, revised ed., Palm Springs, California: ETC Publications, 1979, pp. 1004.

Roer, Berniece, *How to Write Articles*. St. Louis, Missouri: The Bethany Press, 1969, pp. 64.

Stewart, John T., *How to Get Your Church News in Print*. St. Louis: The Bethany Press, 1960, pp. 64.

Strunk, William and E. B. White, *The Elements of Style*, 3rd ed. New York: Macmillan Publishing Company, 1979, pp. 85.

Walker, Robert and others, compilers and editors, *The Successful Writers and Editors Guidebook*. Carol Stream, Illinois: Creation House, 1977, pp. 506.

Wolseley, Roland E., ed., *Writing for the Religious Market*. New York: Association Press, 1956.

About the Author

John A. Moore has been a successful free lance religion writer for over 30 years. Dr. Moore has additionally been a missionary to a number of countries throughout the world and a professor of theology in Switzerland and several seminaries and universities in the United States. Dr. Moore founded the European Baptist Press Service and was the Southern Baptists' Field Representative for all of Europe for seven years.

In addition to having sold over 200 articles, Dr. Moore has written or contributed to half-a-dozen books and has written thousands of news stories and feature articles.

Ordering Information

If you are using a borrowed copy and wish to have a copy of your own, send $9.95 per copy for Write for the Religion Market direct to:

ETC Publications
P.O. Drawer 1627-A
Palm Springs, CA 92263

Your copy will be promptly sent. California residents, please add 6% sales tax.